TRAINING
ENGLISCH

Lesen · Hören · Wortschatz
Sprachmittlung · Schreiben
5. Klasse

Paul Jenkinson

Autor und Illustrator:
Paul Jenkinsons langjährige Berufserfahrung im Unterricht in Deutschland wie auch in seiner Heimat Großbritannien ist ein wichtiger Garant für gute Englisch-Lernhilfen. Mit regelmäßigen Reisen in seine „alte Heimat" verschafft er sich immer wieder einen frischen Eindruck über die aktuell in England diskutierten Themen. Zudem sieht er als Vater eines Sohnes beide Seiten – die des Lehrers wie auch die des Schülers – und versucht, in seiner Arbeit beiden Seiten gerecht zu werden.

© 2016 by Stark Verlagsgesellschaft mbH & Co. KG
www.stark-verlag.de
1. Auflage 2013

Das Werk und alle seine Bestandteile sind urheberrechtlich geschützt. Jede vollständige oder teilweise Vervielfältigung, Verbreitung und Veröffentlichung bedarf der ausdrücklichen Genehmigung des Verlages.

Inhalt

Vorwort
Hinweise zum „ActiveBook"

Reading 1
Topic 1:   Seal Island *(Sachtext)* 2
Topic 2:   Cranberry Hall *(Prospekt)* 5
Topic 3:   The village school *(Verbindung von Text und Bild)* 9
Topic 4:   The ghost train *(Dialog)* 12
Topic 5:   Hi Dave, ... *(E-Mail)* 14
Topic 6:   The Scotsman *(Erzählung)* 17
Topic 7:   I hate shopping! *(Tagebucheintrag)* 21
Topic 8:   Dick Whittington *(Comic)* 24
Topic 9:   Four days in America *(Kleinanzeigen)* 28
Topic 10: Sebastian's problem *(Erzähltext)* 31

Listening 33
Topic 11: No names! *(Dialog und Monolog)* 34
Topic 12: Let's play football – for girls, too *(Gespräch)* 36
Topic 13: Work and school *(Radiointerview)* 39
Topic 14: A short story about eyes *(Erzähltext)* 42
Topic 15: Singleton Hall *(Erzähltext)* 45
Topic 16: The fun-run *(Erfahrungsbericht)* 48
Topic 17: Attention, please! *(Durchsage)* 51
Topic 18: Crime stop *(Radiosendung)* 54
Topic 19: Radio Boston *(Radiosendung)* 57
Topic 20: Answering questions *(Fragen und Antworten)* ... 59
Topic 21: What do you say? *(im Gespräch richtig reagieren)* 61
Topic 22: Kim's party *(Telefongespräch)* 63

Words and Spelling 67
Topic 23: School and the classroom 68
Topic 24: House, home and garden 71

Topic 25:	Colours	81
Topic 26:	The family *(zwei Lückendiktate)*	84
Topic 27:	Clothes *(zwei Diktate)*	90
Topic 28:	Animals and pets	95
Topic 29:	The body *(Diktat)*	99
Topic 30:	British or American English?	103

Mediation ... 107

Topic 31:	A visit to Norfolk *(englische Schilder)*	108
Topic 32:	Can you help me? I don't speak German. *(deutsche Schilder)*	112
Topic 33:	The country teenager *(deutsche Fragen zu englischem Blog)*	115
Topic 34:	My London walk *(E-Mails übertragen)*	117
Topic 35:	Sorry, I don't understand! *(Dolmetschen)*	121
Topic 36:	Student exchange *(Durchsagen erklären)*	123
Topic 37:	School project *(Dialoge übertragen)*	126

Writing ... 129

Topic 38:	Land's End *(Bilder als Schreibanlass, E-Mail)*	130
Topic 39:	Fiona from Scotland *(Verfassen kurzer Geschichten)*	134
Topic 40:	I live here *(Bildbeschreibung)*	137
Topic 41:	An e-mail to … *(E-Mail)*	139
Topic 42:	Some things just happen *(Texte interessanter machen)*	142
Topic 43:	Happy birthday, Luke! *(Bildergeschichte, Formular)*	145
Topic 44:	Free time *(Beiträge für ein Internetforum, Dialog)*	147
Topic 45:	The Eden Project *(Dialoge und Formular)*	154

Vocabulary ... 157

Lösungen zu den Übungsaufgaben ... 183

Bildnachweis ... 273

Die **Audio-Dateien** können direkt im „ActiveBook" abgespielt werden. Zusätzlich enthält die CD alle Audio-Dateien im **MP3-Format**:

Listening
Topic 11: No names! .... Track: 1/2
Topic 12: Let's play football – for girls, too .... Track: 3
Topic 13: Work and school .... Track: 4
Topic 14: A short story about eyes .... Track: 5
Topic 15: Singleton Hall .... Track: 6
Topic 16: The fun-run .... Track: 7
Topic 17: Attention, please! .... Track: 8/9
Topic 18: Crime stop .... Track: 10
Topic 19: Radio Boston .... Track: 11
Topic 20: Answering questions .... Track: 12/13
Topic 21: What do you say? .... Track: 14–17
Topic 22: Kim's party .... Track: 18–20

Words and Spelling
Topic 23: School and the classroom .... Track: 21–23
Topic 24: House, home and garden .... Track: 24–29
Topic 25: Colours .... Track: 30/31
Topic 26: The family .... Track: 32–36
Topic 27: Clothes .... Track: 37–40
Topic 28: Animals and pets .... Track: 41
Topic 29: The body .... Track: 42–45
Topic 30: British or American English? .... Track: 46/47

Mediation
Topic 34: My London walk .... Track: 48
Topic 36: Student exchange .... Track: 49–54
Topic 37: School project .... Track: 55/56

Bitte beachten: Bei der beiliegenden CD handelt es sich um eine CD-ROM, die für den Einsatz am PC optimiert ist. Es ist daher möglich, dass nicht jedes MP3-Abspielgerät die Audio-Dateien erkennt.

Die Hintergrundgeräusche auf der CD stammen aus folgenden Quellen:
freesound, pacdv, Partners in Rhyme, soundsnap

Autor und Illustrator: Paul Jenkinson

Vorwort

Liebe Schülerin, lieber Schüler,

um Englisch gut zu beherrschen, kommt es auf Fertigkeiten wie **Lesen, Hören, Wortschatz, Sprachmittlung** (z. B. einen englischen Text auf Deutsch erklären) und **Schreiben** an. Du kannst sie mit diesem Buch trainieren:

- Jedes Kapitel beginnt mit einer kurzen **Einführung**, in der du erfährst, worauf du z. B. beim Leseverstehen besonders achten solltest. Dann folgen mehrere **Texte** und **Übungen**, die nach und nach schwieriger werden.
- Wenn du noch am Anfang der 5. Klasse bist, solltest du zunächst in jedem Kapitel nur die ersten *Topics* bearbeiten. Wenn du dich schon sicherer fühlst, versuche auch die Übungen mit * zu lösen; sie sind etwas kniffliger.
- In jedem Kapitel werden verschiedene **Tricks und Techniken** vorgestellt, wie du leichter lernen kannst, z. B. wie du dir Wörter besser merkst oder wie du mit bestimmten Aufgabentypen leichter zurechtkommst. Diese Tipps findest du in farbigen Kästen mit dem Titel **„Step up!"**.
- Auf der **CD-ROM** findest du alle Hörverstehenstexte, die du für Übungen in den Kapiteln *Listening, Mediation* und *Words and Spelling* benötigst.
- Selbstverständlich gibt es zu allen Übungen auch **Lösungen**.
- Ebenso enthält das Buch ein **Vokabelverzeichnis**, in dem du die Wörter nachschlagen kannst, die du nicht kennst oder die du vielleicht wieder vergessen hast.
- Mit dem **„ActiveBook"** kannst du das Buch außerdem auf Tablet und PC verwenden. Die **interaktiven Aufgaben** sind ideal zum Üben und Wiederholen geeignet. Mehr dazu findest du in den „Hinweisen zum ‚ActiveBook'".

Du musst dieses Buch nicht von der ersten bis zur letzten Seite durcharbeiten, sondern du kannst …
- immer an dem Thema arbeiten, das ihr gerade im Unterricht behandelt,
- zusätzlich für Klassenarbeiten bzw. Schulaufgaben üben,
- die Kapitel durcharbeiten, mit denen du Schwierigkeiten hast.

Ich wünsche dir viel Spaß und Erfolg bei der Arbeit mit diesem Buch!

Paul Jenkinson

Hinweise zum „ActiveBook"

Über die beiliegende CD oder den Online-Code auf der Umschlaginnenseite erhältst du Zugang zu einer **digitalen Ausgabe** dieses Trainingsbuchs. Im **„ActiveBook"** stehen dir die Inhalte als **elektronischer Text** zur Verfügung. Es bietet dir zudem:

- direkten Zugriff auf die **Audio-Dateien** zu den jeweiligen Aufgaben,
- praktische Links, mit denen du zu den **Lösungen** der Aufgaben gelangst, und
- viele **interaktive Aufgaben**, die du direkt am PC oder Tablet bearbeiten kannst. Diese werden sofort ausgewertet, sodass du gleich eine Rückmeldung erhältst, wie gut du deine Sache gemacht hast.

Achte beim Bearbeiten von Lückentexten im „ActiveBook" darauf, dass du zwischen zwei Wörtern immer nur ein **Leerzeichen** setzt und nicht aus Versehen zwei oder mehr. Den **Apostroph** (wie in *I'm*) erzeugst du, indem du gleichzeitig diese beiden Tasten auf der Tastatur drückst:

Reading –
Strategien zum Kompetenzbereich Leseverstehen

Das Lesen und Verstehen von Texten in einer Fremdsprache ist sehr wichtig. Deshalb solltest du diese Fähigkeiten gerade im ersten Jahr des Englischunterrichts besonders gut einüben. In den Texten wird nur die Grammatik verwendet, die du in der 5. Klasse lernst, und auch die meisten Vokabeln kennst du aus den Schulbüchern. Natürlich wirst du einigen unbekannten Wörtern begegnen, dein Vokabular zu erweitern gehört aber zum Erlernen einer Fremdsprache dazu.

Die Kapitel sind so aufgebaut, dass es dir am besten hilft, wenn du die **vorgegebene Reihenfolge** beachtest. Solltest du Probleme haben, einen Text zu verstehen, könnte es daran liegen, dass er im Augenblick noch zu schwierig für dich ist. Schwierigere Aufgaben sind mit einem Sternchen (*) gekennzeichnet.

- Wenn **Wörter unbekannt** sind, versuche, sie aus dem Zusammenhang zu verstehen. Wenn du nicht weiterkommst, gibt es normalerweise eine Übung, mit der du schwierige Vokabeln lernen kannst. Du kannst auch im Vokabelverzeichnis nachschauen.

- Es gibt verschiedene **Techniken**, die dir helfen, einen Text genau zu verstehen. Sie werden in diesem Kapitel vorgestellt und geübt. Du bekommst außerdem Tipps, wie man bei Aufgabentypen wie z. B. Multiple Choice am besten vorgeht.

- Überprüfe deine Antworten anhand der **Musterlösungen**. Falls du Fehler gemacht hast, versuche herauszufinden warum. Hast du vielleicht die Aufgabe falsch verstanden? Bei vielen Fehlern solltest du die Übungen nach einigen Wochen wiederholen.

Topic 1: Seal Island

1   There are big and small houses on Seal Island. All the houses and their gardens are nice. Kathy, her three children, and their dog, Slipper, live near a river. Peter
5   and Kim are their neighbours. They live near the bridge and they often see Slipper and the children playing in the river.
     The children go to school on the
10 island. Mary's house is on the left of it and Freddy's house is on the right. Jane likes loud music and has no neighbours!
     On the island people buy their food from Harry's small shop. Karen, Tina
15 and Robert live in the three houses near the shop with their families. Robert's got a bike, Tina's got a boat and Karen's got a big garden.

1 Du willst einem Freund oder einer Freundin das Rätsel in Aufgabe 2 erklären, aber du möchtest gerne sicher sein, dass du die folgenden englischen Wörter richtig verstehst.
Lies den Text sorgfältig und schaue dir das Bild des Rätsels an.
Hake (✓) das deutsche Wort ab, das am besten passt.

a) **island**
- [ ] Insel
- [ ] Insekt
- [ ] Ausland

b) **(to) live**
- [ ] lieben
- [ ] lächeln
- [ ] leben

c) **river**
- [ ] Meer
- [ ] Fluss
- [ ] See

d) **neighbour**
- [ ] Nachfolger
- [ ] Nachbarland
- [ ] Nachbar(in)

e) **bridge**
- [ ] Unterführung
- [ ] Brücke
- [ ] Bahnübergang

f) **people**
- [ ] Leute
- [ ] Erwachsene
- [ ] Kinder

2 Sieh dir die Karte von *Seal Island* genau an und vergleiche sie mit dem Text. Schreibe neben die Hausnummern, wer in diesem Haus wohnt.

House Number	Who lives there?
1	
2	
3	
4	
5	
6	
7	
8	
9	

3 In Aufgabe 4 sollst du entscheiden, ob eine Aussage zum Text richtig ist oder nicht. Lies dir diese Aussagen jetzt durch und markiere im Text die Stellen, an denen du Informationen dazu findest. Verwende für jede Aussage eine andere Farbe.

Step up!
- Der Aufgabentyp ***true/false*** kommt sehr häufig vor. Du solltest ihn besonders gut üben.
- Vergleiche die Aussagen genau mit den Textstellen, die du markiert hast. Manchmal klingen die Aussagen ähnlich wie im Text, sind aber doch falsch. ■

4 / Reading

4 Sind die folgenden Sätze richtig *(true)* oder falsch *(false)*?
Mache ein Häkchen (✓) in das passende Kästchen.
Falls ein Satz falsch ist, erkläre warum.

                                                                                               true   false

a) There are one or two nice houses on the island. ☐ ☐

_____

b) Kim lives near children. ☐ ☐

_____

c) Slipper likes water. ☐ ☐

_____

d) Kathy's children have fun in the river. ☐ ☐

_____

e) There isn't a teacher on the island. ☐ ☐

_____

f) Jane listens to quiet music. ☐ ☐

_____

g) Only three people live near the shop. ☐ ☐

_____

h) Karen's neighbour has got a boat. ☐ ☐

_____

5 Beantworte die folgenden Fragen zunächst jeweils nur mit einem Wort.
Schreibe dann einen ganzen Satz, in dem du das Wort verwendest.

a) How many children has Kathy got? *three*
   Kathy has got three children.

b) Who hasn't got a neighbour? _____

_____

c) Is there a big shop on the island? _____

_____

d) Have Harry's neighbours got families? _____

_____

Topic 2: Cranberry Hall

6 Bevor du den Text gründlich liest, sieh ihn dir für eine Minute an. Überfliege den Inhalt nur kurz.

a) Welche Art von Text ist das? _____

b) Woran kannst du das erkennen? _____

c) Finde heraus, um was es ungefähr geht und fasse auf Deutsch zusammen.

_____

6 Reading

7 Verbinde die folgenden Wörter aus dem Text mit der deutschen Bedeutung.

A years old
B (to) open
C until
D adventure playground
E every day

1 bis
2 jeden Tag
3 öffnen
4 Jahre alt
5 Abenteuerspielplatz

A	B	C	D	E

8 Welche der folgenden Aussagen sind richtig *(true)* und welche sind falsch *(false)*?
Hake (✓) das passende Kästchen ab.

> **Step up!**
> Markiere wieder zuerst die wichtigen Textstellen mit verschiedenen Farben. ■

	true	false
a) Cranberry Hall is 249 years old.	☐	☐
b) Cranberry Hall is open on Tuesdays.	☐	☐
c) The adventure playground is new.	☐	☐
d) The museum is open for 9 hours *(Stunden)* every day.	☐	☐
e) The animals are in the gardens.	☐	☐
f) The gardens are not open on Sundays.	☐	☐
g) Cranberry Hall is nice for families.	☐	☐
h) You don't pay to go into the park.	☐	☐

9 Antworte auf die Fragen in ganzen Sätzen.

a) Can you go to Cranberry Hall on a Friday?
_____

b) Is the museum only for old cars?
_____

c) Is the museum or the adventure playground open first?
_____

d) Is the museum open on Sundays?

_____

e) Is there a café at Cranberry Hall?

_____

10 Vervollständige die Sätze.
Verbinde die Satzanfänge (A–F) mit den passenden Satzenden (1–6).

> **Step up!**
> - Es kann sein, dass du bei einer solchen **Zuordnungsaufgabe** zunächst denkst, dass z. B. mehrere Satzteile zu „A" passen.
> - Notiere dann alle Möglichkeiten mit Bleistift. Wenn du alle Teilaufgaben bearbeitet hast, wirst du sehen, dass immer nur zwei Teile zusammenpassen. ■

A At 9 o'clock I can …
B The museum …
C On Thursday I …
D My friends and I …
E We can ride our bikes …
F You can see …

1 can't go to Cranberry Hall.
2 play games in the gardens.
3 in the park.
4 animals in the park.
5 see the old cars.
6 is open on Wednesdays.

A	B	C	D	E	F

11 Lies dir den Text noch einmal durch und sammle alle wichtigen Informationen zu den vorgegebenen Punkten in der Tabelle auf der nächsten Seite.

> **Step up!**
> Es gibt verschiedene Möglichkeiten, mit einem Text zu arbeiten um ihn besser zu verstehen:
> - **Gliederung** in einer Tabelle: Überlege dir Oberbegriffe, zu denen man Informationen im Text findet (du kannst auch deutsche Begriffe verwenden, wenn du das englische Wort noch nicht kennst). Lege eine Tabelle an und sammle alle wichtigen Informationen.
> - **Mindmap:** Schreibe das Thema in die Mitte. Überlege dir Oberbegriffe und zeichne Äste vom Thema zu diesen Begriffen. Zeichne davon aus weitere Äste und notiere die wichtigsten Informationen. ■

8 / Reading

Places in Cranberry Hall	
Opening hours (Öffnungszeiten)	
Price	
Things to see in the museum	
Things to do in the park	

12 Was erfährst du alles über Cranberry Hall in dem Prospekt? Schreibe alles in dieser Mindmap auf. Überlege dir, wie du die Inhalte logisch anordnen kannst.

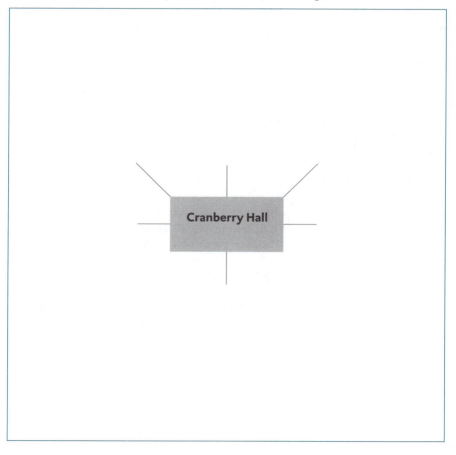

Topic 3: The village school

1   This is a photo of a small school in Scotland. The school is on the Isle of Skye. There are only two classrooms in the school. One teacher lives in the house next to the classrooms. The teacher's neighbour lives in the house behind the school. The other teacher lives in the town 15 miles away.
5   The school has got a school field and a playground. They are not very big because there aren't a lot of children here. The playground is in front of the car on the right. The school field has got a wall and the beach is in front of it.
    The road next to the school is the main road to the village. The village is very small – it has only got twenty houses. The village is about one mile away
10 and the village children walk to school. The other children come by a small bus.

Vocabulary
(to) live in: *wohnen in*
school field: *Sportplatz der Schule*
main road: *Hauptstraße*
behind: *hinter*
playground: *(hier) Schulhof*
beach: *(hier) Küste*

10 Reading

13 Beschrifte die Zeichnung der Schule mit Ausdrücken aus dem Text. Dabei hilft dir die folgende Liste:

(the) teacher's house	(the) beach	(the) main road
(the) school field	(the) classrooms	(the) playground
(the) wall of the school	(the) teacher's neighbour	

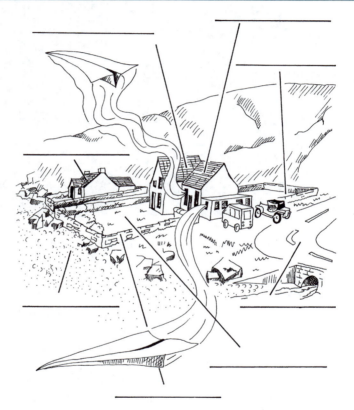

14 Welche der folgenden Aussagen sind richtig *(true)* und welche sind falsch *(false)*? Hake (✓) das passende Kästchen ab.

    true false

a) The school isn't in England. ☐ ☐

b) There are a lot of classrooms in the school. ☐ ☐

c) The teachers live in the houses next to the school. ☐ ☐

d) The playground is small but the school field isn't. ☐ ☐

e) The beach is behind the school. ☐ ☐

f) The road goes to the village. ☐ ☐

g) There is a big village one mile away. ☐ ☐

h) Some children can get a bus to school. ☐ ☐

15 Hake (✓) die richtigen Antworten ab.

> **Step up!**
> Der Aufgabentyp **Multiple Choice** kommt beim Leseverstehen ebenfalls oft vor:
> - Lies immer alle Auswahlmöglichkeiten genau durch und suche die Textstelle, auf die sich die Aussagen beziehen.
> - Vergleiche jede Auswahlmöglichkeit mit dem Text. Hier musst du besonders gut aufpassen, denn manchmal klingen die Möglichkeiten sehr ähnlich. ■

a) You are in the school bus next to the car.
Which is the first building *(Gebäude)*, then the second and then the last?
☐ teacher's house, classrooms, neighbour's house
☐ classrooms, teacher's house, neighbour's house
☐ neighbour's house, teacher's house, classrooms

b) You are looking out of the classroom window.
What is the first thing you see, then the second and then the last?
☐ playground, school field, wall
☐ school field, beach, wall
☐ school field, wall, beach

c) Whose car is in the picture – probably *(wahrscheinlich)*?
☐ the neighbour's car
☐ the teacher's car from the town
☐ a pupil's car

d) It is winter and there is a lot of snow. Who is at school first? Why?
☐ the teacher in the house, because _____
☐ the teacher from the town, because _____
☐ the children from the village, because _____

Topic 4: The ghost train

16 Kirsty und Polly sprechen über die bevorstehende Schulparty.
Allerdings ist der Dialog hier durcheinander geraten. Kannst du ihn in die richtige Reihenfolge bringen?
Der Anfang ist bereits vorgegeben. Fülle die Tabelle aus.

A KIRSTY: It's different this year, Polly. It's great. There's a ghost of an old woman. She stands next to you, then she tells you a terrible story – a story about a big fire in the school in 1847. At the end of the story a skeleton pushes you away. Then there's the man without a head and some other things, but the old woman, she's so real – it's very scary, Polly.

B POLLY: Oh no, not again. Mr Black and 5 C always have a ghost train. The first time you see it, it's very good but then after that it's always the same.

C KIRSTY: Cool! That's scary.

D (Polly goes on the ghost train)

E KIRSTY: The ghost train. 5 C have got a ghost train in their classroom. It's for the school party.

F POLLY: Kirsty, there isn't an old woman – every year it's the same!

G POLLY: What's scary, Kirsty?

H KIRSTY: But ... the old woman, Polly? Isn't she great?

I POLLY: It's boring. Last year – this year – next year – it's always the same; a skeleton, the man without a head and some other things.

1	2	3	4	5	6	7	8	9
C								

17 Bist du sicher, dass du die folgenden englischen Wörter richtig verstehst?
Wähle das deutsche Wort aus, das am besten passt und mache ein Häkchen (✓).

a) **ghost train** ☐ Geisterbahn
☐ U-Bahn
☐ Fahrbahn

b) **scary** ☐ süß
☐ aufregend
☐ furchterregend

c) **(the) same** ☐ anderes
☐ Gegenteil
☐ derselbe (die-/das-)

d) **skeleton** ☐ Knochen
☐ Skelett
☐ Körper

e) **without** ☐ ohne   f) **real** ☐ echt/real
          ☐ mit   ☐ wirklich
          ☐ aus   ☐ falsch

18 Vervollständige die Antworten zu folgenden Fragen. Sieh in der Lösung nach, wenn du den Text nochmals in der richtigen Reihenfolge lesen möchtest.

a) Who has got the ghost train? _____ have got the ghost train.

b) Where is the ghost train? The ghost train is in their _____.

c) Who is 5 C's teacher? _____ is 5 C's teacher.

d) What is the old woman? The old woman is a _____.

e) What pushes you away? A _____ pushes you away.

f) What hasn't the man got? The man hasn't got a _____.

19 Kannst du mit der Geisterbahn fahren, ohne dich zu verirren? Verbinde alle Buchstaben deiner Antworten von Aufgabe 18 a–f und du findest den Ausgang.

20 Beantworte die folgenden Fragen in ganzen Sätzen. Schreibe in dein Heft.

a) Who is Kirsty talking to?

b) Why have 5 C got a ghost train in their classroom?

c) What is the problem with the ghost train?

d) What is the old woman's story?

e) Polly goes on the ghost train. But what isn't there?

Topic 5: Hi Dave, ...

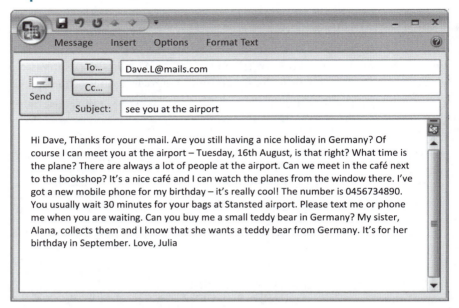

Hi Dave, Thanks for your e-mail. Are you still having a nice holiday in Germany? Of course I can meet you at the airport – Tuesday, 16th August, is that right? What time is the plane? There are always a lot of people at the airport. Can we meet in the café next to the bookshop? It's a nice café and I can watch the planes from the window there. I've got a new mobile phone for my birthday – it's really cool! The number is 0456734890. You usually wait 30 minutes for your bags at Stansted airport. Please text me or phone me when you are waiting. Can you buy me a small teddy bear in Germany? My sister, Alana, collects them and I know that she wants a teddy bear from Germany. It's for her birthday in September. Love, Julia

Vocabulary
(to) meet: *treffen*

21 Julia war sehr in Eile als sie die E-Mail schrieb und hat daher alle Absätze weggelassen. In welche sinnvollen Abschnitte könnte man den Text gliedern? Zeichne ein, wo eine neue Zeile beginnen sollte.

22 Sieh dir die Bilder auf der nächsten Seite genau an.
Welche Wörter für Dinge oder Orte aus der E-Mail passen zum Bild? Schreibe jeweils das englische und das deutsche Wort zu den Fotos.

23 Hake (✓) die richtigen Kästchen ab.

a) Dave is …
☐ working in Germany.
☐ having a holiday in Germany.
☐ living in Germany.

b) Dave asks Julia to meet him on …
☐ Monday.
☐ Tuesday.
☐ Wednesday.

c) Where can Dave find Julia?

A ☐   B ☐   C ☐

16 ◆ Reading

d) Dave waits for … for his bags.
☐ a quarter of an hour
☐ half an hour
☐ one hour

e) Does Julia like her present?
☐ Yes, she does.
☐ No, she doesn't.
☐ She hasn't got a present.

f) Does Julia's sister have a lot of teddy bears?
☐ Yes, she does.
☐ No, she doesn't.
☐ The answer isn't in the e-mail.

24 Beantworte die folgenden Fragen in ganzen Sätzen.

a) Where is Dave?
_____

b) Does Julia meet Tom?
_____

c) Can Julia buy something to read at the airport?
_____

d) How big is Alana's present?
_____

e) Are the sisters' birthdays in September?
_____

25 Dave ist am Flughafen angekommen. Er schickt Julia eine Nachricht. Vervollständige die Lücken mit Wörtern aus der E-Mail.

I'm _____ for my two _____.
Are you in the _____?
I've got the _____ for your _____.
Oh, here come my _____ now!
Dave

Topic 6: The Scotsman

1. Bang! "Not again," Duffy thinks. Bang! Bang! Bang! Then the noises stop. This time Duffy picks up his camera from the table in his bedroom and goes downstairs. He opens the living-room door and sees a man. The man's big – two metres – and
5. he's wearing a kilt. The man looks at Duffy.
   "Bread! Water!" he shouts.
   Duffy wants to take a photo of the man but the Scotsman shouts again, "Bread! Water!"
   Duffy goes to the kitchen and brings back some bread
10. and water. The big man eats and drinks. The Scotsman then looks at Duffy and says, "Run! They're looking for us."
   "Who are?" Duffy asks.
   "The English," answers the man. "We must run away."
   "Why? What's the matter?" asks Duffy.
15. "Culloden. Listen! Somebody is coming – it's the English. Run!" says the Scotsman. "We have to go, now!"
   Duffy watches the Scotsman open the door and run away. Then Duffy hears somebody coming and he goes outside.
   "Good morning, Duffy," Mrs Macdonald says. "Can't you sleep this
20. morning? Here's your newspaper."
   "What's the date today, Mrs Macdonald?" asks Duffy.
   "How can you forget that? 16th April – a bad day for Scotland, a very bad day!"

Vocabulary
Culloden: *berühmte Schlacht zwischen Engländern und Schotten am 16.4.1746, die die Engländer gewannen*

26 Verbinde die Wörter aus dem Text mit der richtigen deutschen Bedeutung.

A	downstairs	1	ein Foto machen
B	kilt	2	Zeitung
C	bread	3	nach unten
D	(to) take a photo	4	Brot
E	Scotsman	5	Schottenrock
F	newspaper	6	Schotte

A	B	C	D	E	F

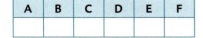

18 / Reading

*27 Lies dir den Text noch einmal genau durch und überlege dir fünf Fragen zum Inhalt. Du darfst aber keine Fragen übernehmen, die schon im Text stehen. Verwende Fragen mit *what? why? who? where?* oder *how ...?*

a) _____

b) _____

c) _____

d) _____

e) _____

28 Jede der folgenden Fragen wird durch eine der drei Zeichnungen beantwortet. Mache ein Häkchen (✓) bei der richtigen Zeichnung.

a) Where is Duffy's camera?

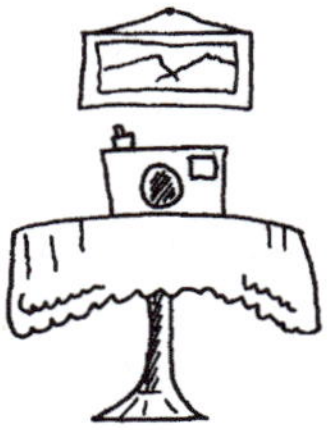

A 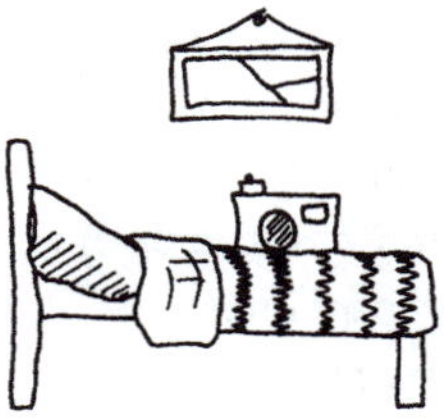 ☐   B  ☐   C ☐

b) Which man is the Scotsman?

A  ☐   B  ☐   C ☐

c) Which room is the man in?

A  ☐   B  ☐   C ☐

Topic 6: The Scotsman   19

d) What does Duffy bring the Scotsman?

A ☐   B ☐   C ☐

e) Who is looking for the Scotsman?

A ☐   B ☐   C ☐

f) Who is Mrs Macdonald?

A ☐   B ☐   C ☐

29 Sind die Aussagen richtig *(true)* oder falsch *(false)*?
Wähle das passende Kästchen aus. Korrigiere alle falschen Aussagen.

	true	false
a) Duffy hears the man for the first time.	☐	☐
b) The man is in the kitchen.	☐	☐
c) The man is from Scotland.	☐	☐

d) Duffy takes a good photo of the man. ☐ ☐

e) The English are chasing the man. ☐ ☐

f) The Scotsman hears Mrs Macdonald. ☐ ☐

g) Mrs Macdonald brings the evening newspaper. ☐ ☐

h) Duffy forgets which day it is, today. ☐ ☐

i) 16th April is a lucky day for Scotland. ☐ ☐

j) The Scotsman is a ghost. ☐ ☐

30 Beantworte die folgenden Fragen in ganzen Sätzen.

a) Where do the noises come from?

b) Describe *(beschreiben)* the Scotsman.

c) What does the man want?

d) Why does the Scotsman run away?

31 Was geschah bevor der Text beginnt? Wähle die beste Beschreibung aus.
☐ A man takes photos of a ghost.
☐ There is a battle *(Schlacht)*.
☐ A man often hears noises in his house.

Topic 7: I hate shopping!

Dear diary,

I have to go shopping with my mum today. She's buying me new clothes for school. I hate shopping with her. She always buys things too big: shirts, trousers, pullovers and shoes. "You can grow into them," she says, and then the things are never the right things – they aren't what my friends wear. "I'm not buying a pair of training shoes for £155," she says. "These are only £15. You can have those."

She doesn't understand that you have to wear the right clothes in school. I don't know why I have to go shopping with her. She never buys me what I want and everything is blue and everything is too big. I could go cycling or play football or something. I'm not going this time. I'm staying here.

> **Step up!**
> Überlege auch hier wieder, welche Art von Text das ist und woran du dies erkennen kannst. ■

Sam hears his mother shouting, "Sam, are you ready? We're going to Peter's Sports, they've got a sale today."

"But the sports shop in George Street has got better training shoes," Sam answers.

"Peter's sale is good enough for school, Sam."

"But I want something nice, Mum."

"You always get nice things – things that you can grow into."

22 Reading

32 Lies den Text sorgfältig und wähle das deutsche Wort aus, das am besten passt.

a) **(to) have to**
- [ ] hassen
- [ ] müssen
- [ ] brauchen

b) **(to) grow into**
- [ ] in etwas hineinwachsen
- [ ] hineinbringen
- [ ] größer werden

c) **(to) go cycling**
- [ ] Ski fahren
- [ ] fahren
- [ ] Fahrrad fahren

d) **sale**
- [ ] Schlussverkauf
- [ ] segeln
- [ ] kaufen

e) **better**
- [ ] gut
- [ ] besser
- [ ] schlechter

f) **enough**
- [ ] viele
- [ ] wenige
- [ ] genug

33 Verbinde den Anfang jedes Satzes (A–F) mit dem richtigen Ende (1–6). So ergeben sich sechs neue Sätze über den Text. Schreibe die neuen Sätze auf.

A Sam doesn't like ...
B Sam needs ...
C Sam's mother doesn't ...
D Sam wants ...
E They are going to one shop ...
F Sam thinks ...

1 what his friends have got.
2 because it has got a sale.
3 the shop in George Street is good.
4 buy expensive training shoes for school.
5 shopping with his mum.
6 some new school clothes.

A	B	C	D	E	F
5					

Sam doesn't like shopping with his mum.

34 Sam träumt davon, mit seiner Mutter einkaufen zu gehen. Wenn seine Tagträume wahr würden, würden sie ihn glücklich oder traurig machen?
Schreibe über jeden Tagtraum ein großes ‚H' für ‚happy' (glücklich) oder ein ‚S' für ‚sad' (traurig).

Topic 8: Dick Whittington

35 Verbinde die folgenden Wörter des Comics mit den richtigen deutschen Wörtern.

A made of   1 *Mäuse*
B (to) come with 2 *Boot/Schiff*
C cart   3 *aus*
D nowhere   4 *reich*
E mice   5 *nirgendwo*
F boat   6 *unglücklich*
G unhappy   7 *mitkommen*
H rich   8 *Wagen*

A	B	C	D	E	F	G	H

36 Welche der folgenden Aussagen sind richtig *(true)* und welche sind falsch *(false)*? Verbessere alle falschen Aussagen.

                                                                true false

a) Dick doesn't like where he lives.   ☐   ☐

b) Dick goes to London in the afternoon.   ☐   ☐

c) A man takes him to London.   ☐   ☐

d) Dick is happy in London.   ☐   ☐

e) Dick has no friends so he buys a cat.   ☐   ☐

f) Mr Fitzwarren buys clothes from the Sultan.   ☐   ☐

g) There are usually mice on the boat.   ☐   ☐

h) The cat stays with Dick. ☐ ☐
_____

i) There are no cats in Barbary. ☐ ☐
_____

j) The money comes from Mr Fitzwarren. ☐ ☐
_____

***37** Kannst du dich noch genau an den Inhalt des Comics erinnern?
Ein Teil davon steht hier als Geschichte, aber es fehlen einige Wörter.
Versuche, die fehlenden Wörter zu ergänzen, ohne den Comicstrip noch einmal zu lesen.

In London, Dick has got _____ to sleep. Mrs Fitzwarren gives him _____ and somewhere to _____. But there are mice in his _____. Dick _____ a cat and the cat _____ the mice.
Then, Mr Fitzwarren tells Dick about the _____ on his boat.
Dick gives Mr Fitzwarren his _____
and very soon there are no mice on the _____.
In Barbary, the Sultan is very _____
because there are mice everywhere there, too.
Mr Fitzwarren gives the Sultan
_____ cat.
Dick's cat then eats all
the mice in _____
and the Sultan is
_____ again.
The Sultan sends Dick a _____ to say thank you.
The Sultan's present makes Dick a _____ man.

Topic 9: Four days in America

38 Tom, Mary, Jason und Tina sind mit ihren Eltern in den Ferien in den USA. Jeder darf für einen Tagesausflug einen besonderen Wunsch äußern.
In einem Prospekt lesen sie diese Kleinanzeigen für Sehenswürdigkeiten.

A) Muir Woods

Visit Muir Woods about one hour north of San Francisco. Here you can see lots of Redwood trees.

Redwood trees are very old and tall. One tree is 258 feet tall; that's about 79 metres!

There are also lots of forest plants and animals to see.

B) DINOSAUR LAND

Here you can see the footprints of dinosaurs. There are lots of them. You can see dinosaur eggs, too. You can walk with a Native American and he shows you where the footprints are and tells you about them.

C) THE GOLDEN GATE BRIDGE

The bridge is open every day. You can park near the bridge and then walk onto it.

It is open for people from 5 a.m. until 9 p.m.

You can also use a bike from our shop to ride on it.

There are fantastic views of San Francisco from the bridge.

D) Venice Beach

Visit the famous Venice Beach: sea, sand, palm trees, people skateboarding, rollerblading, cycling and jogging. There are lots of small shops, cafés and interesting houses, too. Sometimes you see famous people here or somebody making a film.

E) Highway 1

The most beautiful road in America. Drive along the coast from San Francisco to Los Angeles. See the fantastic coast and the birds that live here. Stop at Pismo Beach and watch the pelicans fly above your head.

Die Eltern der Kinder waren vor einigen Jahren schon einmal in den USA und haben viele Fotos gemacht. Suche die Fotos, die zu den Anzeigen passen.
Zu einem Foto gibt es keine Anzeige. Fülle die Tabelle aus.

A	B	C	D	E

39 Die Kinder erklären, was sie interessiert und was sie sehen wollen.
Suche für jede Person die passende Sehenswürdigkeit aus und schreibe sie in die richtige Sprechblase.

Tom		"I like films and I hope I can see a famous person sometime on our holiday. I want to swim in the sea where it's warm. But I want to go somewhere that's fun – where there is lots to do and see."
Mary		"I don't like big towns and cities. I want to go somewhere quiet. I want to see the countryside; the trees, the animals, the plants and the flowers. I don't want to see houses, shops and lots of cars and people."
Tina		"I like buildings but I want to see something that is famous and that everybody knows. There are always lots of photos about famous places in our books at school and I want to see one of them."
Jason		"Beaches are boring! Shops, too. I want to see something different. I like animals. Big animals – very big animals – monster animals! I read a lot of books about millions of years ago on our planet and sometimes I visit museums, too. But, here the animals are real – well, almost!"

Topic 10: Sebastian's problem

1. "Okay children. Today is our first English lesson together. I'm Miss Roberts and I want you to write about your house," the teacher says and then she writes the title on the blackboard. Miss Roberts is new and doesn't know many of the children. She tells them that they can write about how many bedrooms their house has got, or about the garden for example, but they have to give lots of details.

2. Sebastian doesn't want to write about his house. He asks his teacher, "Can I write about sport or a television programme?" but his teacher says "no". Sebastian thinks and then starts to write about his house. *'I don't live in the town. I live in a house in the country. It has got lots of bedrooms, living rooms, windows and doors. Outside there is a garden.'*

3. The teacher sees what Sebastian is writing. She isn't very happy and tells him that he has to write more and give a lot more details, like how many bedrooms it has got. She also tells him that people don't have living rooms.

4. "But that's just one of my problems and this is why I want to write about sport or television," Sebastian wants to say. After one or two minutes he starts his story again.
'I live in a very big house in the country and we don't have any neighbours. The house is over 300 years old. It's got 15 bedrooms and 17 rooms downstairs. It has got, for example, a summer living room, a winter living room and a morning room. We have also got a big park with lots of animals, a lake and a church in it. There are four gardens, too. A rose garden, a fruit garden, a vegetable garden and a garden in front of the house.'

5. His teacher looks at Sebastian's story. "Sebastian," she says, "It's a very good story and it's got lots of details in it but you have to write about your house – not a fantasy house." Sebastian isn't very happy but his friend, Jenny, asks Miss Roberts, "Can I talk to you outside please?" They go outside together. Jenny then explains to her teacher what Sebastian's problem is – he really does live in this very, very big house and it's embarrassing for him.

6. Jenny and the teacher go back into the classroom. She tells Sebastian that she understands everything now and likes his story but then Jimmy Jones shouts "That's not fair! He can write about a fantasy house and I can't. I want to write a fantasy story, too – my house is boring!"
"Oh no," Miss Roberts thinks: "What next?"

Vocabulary
detail: *Detail, Einzelheit;* fruit: *Obst;* embarrassing: *peinlich*

32 / Reading

*40 Die Geschichte ist in sechs Absätze unterteilt. Jeder Absatz braucht eine Überschrift. Welche der unten stehenden Überschriften passt zu welchem Teil der Geschichte? Fülle die Tabelle aus.
Eine Überschrift fehlt. Du musst dir deine eigene Überschrift für diesen Teil ausdenken und sie in die Lücke schreiben.

Story part	Heading
	Jenny saves the day
	Sebastian's story
	Miss Roberts is angry
	One problem after the other
	The boring story

41 Sieh die Bilder an. Ordne jedem Teil der Geschichte ein passendes Bild zu.

1	2	3	4	5	6

Listening –
Strategien zum Kompetenzbereich Hörverstehen

Es gibt verschiedene **Arten von Hörverstehenstexten**, z. B. Dialoge, Monologe oder kurze Durchsagen. Dieses Kapitel enthält Texte aus all diesen Bereichen. Du findest jeweils einfachere und schwierigere Texte zu jeder Textsorte. Schwierigere Aufgaben sind wieder mit einem Sternchen (*) gekennzeichnet.

- Am Anfang jedes *Topics* stehen einige Wörter oder Namen, die du vielleicht noch nicht kennst. Mache die **Vokabelübungen**, bevor du dir den Text zum ersten Mal anhörst. Dann kennst du die neuen Wörter schon.

- Lies die Übungen sorgfältig, sodass du sie wirklich verstehst. Sollte in den Aufgaben einmal ein Wort vorkommen, das du noch nicht kennst, kannst du es im Vokabelverzeichnis am Ende des Bandes nachschlagen.

- Zur Übung kannst du dir die Hörverstehenstexte ruhig so oft anhören wie du möchtest. Versuche dich langsam zu steigern und die Zahl der Wiederholungen nach und nach zu reduzieren. Sollte in einem Test oder einer Klassenarbeit Hörverstehen vorkommen, so werden dir die Texte meist zweimal vorgespielt.

- Weitere Tipps, wie du am besten bei der Bearbeitung von Hörverstehensaufgaben vorgehst, findest du direkt neben den Übungen (**„Step up!"**).

Topic 11: No names!

42 Track 1

Der Lehrer will einige Bilder zurückgeben, aber es stehen keine Namen darauf. Chloe sagt, dass sie weiß, wer die Bilder gemalt hat. Jetzt ist gerade Pause und sie hilft bei der Zuordnung.
Höre dir das Gespräch zwischen Chloe und ihrem Lehrer an.
Wer hat welches Bild gemalt? Mache ein Häkchen (✓), wenn du weißt, dass die Information stimmt, und ein Kreuz (✗), wenn sie falsch ist.

> **Step up!**
> - Sieh dir die Tabelle vor dem Hören genau an.
> - Höre dir den Text an. Achte besonders auf Informationen zu den Begriffen, die in der Tabelle stehen.
> - Höre ihn dir ein zweites Mal an und löse die Aufgabe.
> - Höre dir den Text noch ein letztes Mal an und überprüfe deine Lösung.
> - Nur wenn du große Schwierigkeiten hast, den Text zu verstehen, kannst du ihn zusätzlich noch durchlesen. Du findest ihn im Lösungsteil zu Beginn von *Topic 11*. ∎

	fish	car	people in a disco	people in a park	water
Chloe					
Laura					
Jenny					
Robert					
Mike					

Topic 11: No names! / 35

*43 Kannst du dich erinnern, worüber Chloe und der Lehrer gesprochen haben? Vervollständige die Lücken in folgendem Text. (*painted* = hat gemalt)

There are no _____ on the pictures. Chloe is helping her _____. Chloe's help _____ very good. Chloe says Mike's _____ painted a _____. She is Chloe's _____. Chloe then _____ the teacher who painted the people in the _____. The teacher can now _____ the pictures back to the children.

44 Chloes Kunstlehrerin sagt ihren Schülern, wo sie ihre Bilder an die Wand hängen sollen. Schreibe das Thema jedes Bildes in den richtigen Bilderrahmen.

Track 2

Topic 12: Let's play football – for girls, too

45 Falls es im Text einige Wörter gibt, die du nicht kennst, ist das nicht schlimm. Du kannst trotzdem die Bedeutung aus dem Zusammenhang verstehen. Es kommen jedoch fünf neue Wörter vor, die du lernen solltest, bevor du den Text zum ersten Mal anhörst.
Ordne das deutsche Wort der richtigen englischen Bedeutung zu.
Schreibe es an die richtige Stelle.

| etwas | typisch | Witz | unfair | müssen |

a) joke   A <u>joke</u> is a funny story.   _____
b) not fair   It's <u>not fair</u> when you do all the work. _____
c) something   Can we do <u>something</u> for the party?   _____
d) have to   You <u>have to</u> go to school.   _____
e) typical   That's <u>typical</u>! They're always late.   _____

46 Max, Wendy und einige andere Schüler der 5 b müssen ihr Klassenzimmer für ein Schulfest vorbereiten. Aber nicht jeder ist rechtzeitig da.
Höre was geschieht und wähle die richtigen Antworten aus.

Track 3

Step up!
- Lies dir die Fragen vor dem Hören sorgfältig durch und sieh dir die Bilder an. Nur eines ist jeweils richtig.
- Höre dir den Text an und mache ein Häkchen bei den Antworten, die du schon sicher weißt.
- Die Fragen stehen in der richtigen Reihenfolge, d. h., du merkst, wenn du eine Antwort verpasst.
- Falls du unsicher bist, versuche es andersherum: suche zuerst die Antworten, die falsch sind. ■

a) Where is Tony?

A ☐   B ☐   C ☐

b) What must the pupils do?

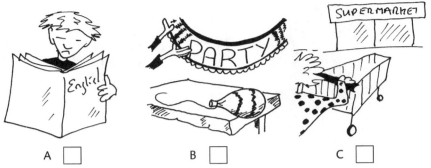

A ☐   B ☐   C ☐

c) Who takes the bag?

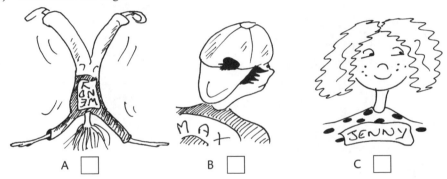

A ☐   B ☐   C ☐

d) What is Tony's idea?

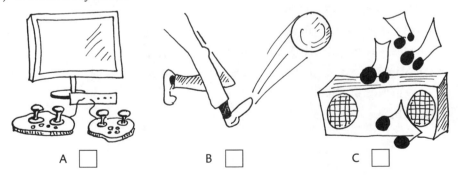

A ☐   B ☐   C ☐

e) What isn't in the classroom?

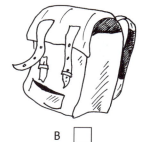
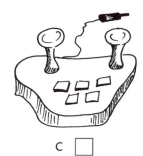

A ☐ B ☐ C ☐

*47 Vervollständige die Lücken in der Geschichte.

> **Step up!**
> - Der **Lückentext** stimmt nicht genau mit dem Hörtext überein. Es handelt sich eher um eine Zusammenfassung der Handlung.
> - Versuche dich an die wichtigsten Dinge zu erinnern und fülle die Lücken. Falls nötig, kannst du dir den Text auch nochmals anhören. ■

The boys and _____ have to make their classroom _____ for a _____. Max is in the _____ and then Wendy _____. She asks where the other _____ are.

She is angry (= *böse*) because the boys are _____ computer games. She and her _____, Jenny, take Tony's _____. When Tony arrives, he is angry _____ the girls aren't there. He thinks the boys always have to do all the _____. He tells Max to get his ball, then they can play _____. His ball is in the bag. But his _____ isn't there.

Topic 13: Work and school

48 Einige Wörter werden im nächsten Text neu für dich sein. Mache diese Übung und lerne die Wörter bevor du den Text zum ersten Mal hörst.
Ordne die englischen Wörter der passenden Abbildung und der richtigen deutschen Übersetzung zu. Fülle die Tabelle aus.

> Zeitungen – sich fertig machen – festhalten – Sendung – aufwachen – (Zeitungen) austragen

Englisch	Bild	Deutsch	Englisch	Bild	Deutsch
programme			(to) deliver		
(to) hold			newspapers		
(to) wake up			(to) get ready		

49 Johns Klasse macht eine Radiosendung über Schüler und ihre Nebenjobs.
John arbeitet gerade und Sally nimmt auf, was er sagt.
Höre dir an, was John über seine Arbeit erzählt.

> **Step up!**
> - Da John draußen ist, als er spricht, gibt es hier **Hintergrundgeräusche**. Versuche, dich davon nicht ablenken zu lassen.
> - Um dich daran zu gewöhnen, kannst du den Text zur Übung ruhig häufiger anhören. ■

a) Wann tut John all das?
Verbinde, was John tut, mit der richtigen Zeit. Nicht alle Zeiten und Handlungen werden verwendet.

b) Schreibe einen Satz zu jeder Handlung. Sage auch, wann diese geschieht.

At _____ John wakes up.

At _____
_____
_____
_____
_____

Topic 13: Work and school 41

50 Höre dir das Gespräch noch einmal an.
Beantworte jede Frage mit **einem** Wort oder **einer** Zahl.

a) How old is John? _____
b) Is John near Mr Grey's house? _____
c) Who is working? _____
d) Is it a nice morning? _____
e) Is Sally happy? _____
f) Does John wake up late? _____
g) What does John do before he goes to the shop? _____
h) When does John like his job? _____
i) How does John go to school? _____
j) What is the king's name? _____
k) Does John eat his dinner before he does his homework? _____
l) Has John got a computer? _____
m) Does John work at weekends? _____

51 Sieh dir das Bild genau an. Kreise mindestens fünf Fehler ein, die darauf zu sehen sind. Schreibe, warum du etwas eingekreist hast.

- _____
- _____
- _____
- _____
- _____

Topic 14: A short story about eyes

52 Jeder Satz enthält ein Wort aus dem Text, das du vielleicht noch nicht kennst. Dieses Wort ist **fett** gedruckt. Welches deutsche Wort aus der Liste hat dieselbe Bedeutung wie das englische Wort?

> schnell dunkel sicher
> Angst haben bis jemand

a) It is **dark** at 11.30 in the evening. _____

b) Can **somebody** help me, please? _____

c) I am **frightened** of snakes. _____

d) He reads **until** 7 o'clock. _____

e) She can run **quickly**. _____

f) Your money is **safe** in a bank. _____

53 Höre dir die Geschichte über Steves und Janes abenteuerlichen Heimweg an.
Notiere während des Hörens alle Begriffe, die dir wichtig erscheinen.
Achte darauf, nicht zu viel aufzuschreiben.

Track 5

> **Step up!**
> - Mit einer solchen Übung findest du heraus, worum es insgesamt in einem Text geht.
> - Auch wenn dir ein Hörtext schwierig erscheint, wirst du sicher einige Wörter verstehen. Notiere diese Begriffe und versuche, daraus den Zusammenhang zu erschließen.
> - Du wirst sehen, nach dieser Vorübung kannst du auch schwierigere Hörtexte verstehen.

Beispiel:

Hörtext: "It's November and it's late in the evening."

Schlüsselwörter, die du notieren könntest: ___November, late, evening___

Verwende dann die notierten englischen Wörter und sage auf Deutsch, worum es in der Geschichte ungefähr geht.

Topic 14: A short story about eyes | 43

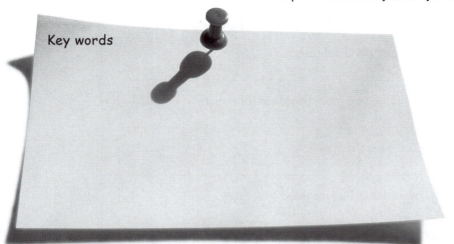

Key words

Worum geht es in der Geschichte?

_____
_____
_____
_____

54 Höre dir die Geschichte noch einmal an. Welche Aussagen sind richtig *(true)* und welche sind falsch *(false)*? Hake (✓) das passende Kästchen ab.
Ist eine Aussage falsch, so schreibe die richtige Aussage aus dem Text auf.

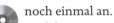
Track 5

Step up!
- Auch beim Hörverstehen kommt **true/false** oft vor.
- Lies dir alle Aussagen gründlich durch, bevor du dir den Text anhörst.
- Überlege während des Hörens genau, ob eine Aussage richtig oder falsch ist.
- Du kannst dir während des Hörens auch zu jeder Aussage wichtige Schlüsselwörter aus dem Text notieren (auf einem Notizzettel) und danach entscheiden, ob die Aussage richtig oder falsch ist. Wird von dir verlangt, dass du falsche Aussagen korrigierst, so kannst du dazu deine Notizen verwenden.
- Die Aussagen stehen in der Reihenfolge, in der sie im Text behandelt werden. ■

Listening

		true	false
a)	The party is in summer.	☐	☐
b)	There are two more people in the street.	☐	☐
c)	Steve sees the eyes first.	☐	☐
d)	Jane doesn't like the eyes.	☐	☐
e)	Jane sees the eyes in the house.	☐	☐
f)	The people run home.	☐	☐
g)	Steve closes the door.	☐	☐
h)	There is a cat in the tree.	☐	☐

55 Der Comic erzählt die Geschichte von Steve und Jane. Vervollständige den Text dafür.

Topic 15: Singleton Hall

56 Kennst du die **fett** gedruckten englischen Wörter in den folgenden Sätzen? Lies die Möglichkeiten sorgfältig durch und hake (✓) das deutsche Wort ab, das deiner Meinung nach am besten zu dem englischen Wort passt.

a) I walk **towards** the tree.
- [ ] nach
- [ ] in Richtung
- [ ] über

b) We **live** in a big old house.
- [ ] schlafen
- [ ] arbeiten
- [ ] wohnen

c) The children **run away** from the woman.
- [ ] weglaufen
- [ ] gehen
- [ ] kommen

d) It is a **strange** story about the children.
- [ ] lustig
- [ ] merkwürdig
- [ ] fröhlich

e) Mary's photo is here. Her name is on the **back** of it.
- [ ] Vorderseite
- [ ] Rückseite
- [ ] Seite

f) The old house has got a **ghost**.
- [ ] Clown
- [ ] Hund
- [ ] Gespenst

57 Carols Familie wohnt seit 400 Jahren in Singleton Hall.
Eines Tages erschrickt Carol sehr: Sie trifft zwei ihrer Vorfahren.
Höre, was geschieht.
Hake (✓) das richtige Kästchen ab oder schreibe die Antwort auf.
Du musst keine ganzen Sätze schreiben, einzelne Wörter oder Ziffern genügen.

a) Which house is Singleton Hall?

A ☐   B ☐   C ☐

b) Where is the ball?

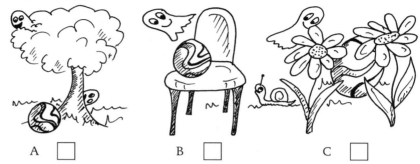

A ☐   B ☐   C ☐

c) How many children are there? _____

d) Who talks to Carol first? _____

e) What is Chris doing?

A ☐   B ☐   C ☐

f) When does Chris see the children? _____

g) Which photo are they looking at?

A ☐   B ☐   C ☐

h) What are the children? _____

58 Kannst du die Geschichte erzählen? Erinnere dich an das, was du gerade gehört hast, und vervollständige den Lückentext.

Carol lives in an _____ house. Today she is in the _____. She sees two _____ and talks to them. Then they _____ from Carol. Carol then _____ her brother about the children in the garden. Her brother is _____ at some old _____. Chris shows them to Carol. He asks her to read the _____ of one photograph. Chris thinks the children are _____.

59 Schreibe das richtige Wort aus dem Text in das Rätsel.
a) Which day is it?
b) The month.
c) Carol tells Chris a _____.
d) _____ twelve.
e) Where is the house?
f) What is Chris sitting on?
g) What are the boy and girl doing?

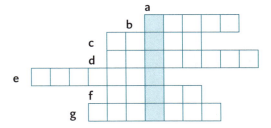

Topic 16: The fun-run

60 Kennst du die folgenden englischen Wörter?
Markiere das deutsche Wort, das deiner Meinung nach am besten passt.

fun-run	*Spaziergang*	*Langlauf*	*Wohltätigkeitslauf*
around	*über*	*unter*	*um ... herum*
message	*Massage*	*Nachricht*	*Nachrichten*
years old	*Alter*	*Jubiläum*	*Jahre alt*
farm	*Bahnhof*	*Bauernhof*	*Tiergarten*
doctor	*Arzt, Ärztin*	*Mechaniker(in)*	*Maler(in)*

61 Vervollständige nun jeden Satz mit einem der neuen Wörter.

a) There is a _____ at school to get money for poor (= *arm*) people.

b) My leg hurts. I must go to the _____.

c) I am 12 _____.

d) There are lots of animals on the _____.

e) There is a _____ for you from Tina.

f) We must run _____ the school.

62 Im Unterricht geht es heute um ein Dorf in Afrika. Du hörst einen kurzen Bericht und was der Lehrer dazu sagt.
Beantworte die Fragen mit einzelnen Wörtern oder Ziffern.

Track 7

a) Who runs?
- _____
- _____

b) How old is Karani? _____

c) How many other children are in Karani's family?
_____

d) What are Karani's favourite lessons (= *Lieblingsfächer*) in school?
- _____
- _____

e) How many classrooms are there in the school? _____

f) How many pupils go to the school?
_____

g) Have Karani's parents got a shop?
_____

h) Has the family got a lot of money?
_____

i) How many rooms has Karani's house got?
_____

j) Is there a bus to Karani's village?
_____

k) Is there a doctor in her village?
_____

63 Woran kannst du dich erinnern? Hake (✓) die richtigen Kästchen ab.

	true	false
a) Park School is in Africa.	☐	☐
b) The fun-run is at school.	☐	☐
c) The teacher reads Karani's e-mail.	☐	☐
d) Karani's class is big.	☐	☐
e) Karani can walk to a doctor.	☐	☐
f) The water is not in Karani's village.	☐	☐
g) Karani works after school.	☐	☐
h) The money goes to Karani's family.	☐	☐
i) The teacher hasn't got the photos with him today.	☐	☐

50 Listening

***64** Nun zeigt der Lehrer den Schülern einige Fotos von Karanis Dorf.
Höre dir den Text noch einmal an. Hake (✓) die Fotos ab, die einen Aspekt von Karanis Leben zeigen. Beschreibe die ausgewählten Fotos.

Track 7

Foto	Passt zu Karani	Beschreibung
A		
B		
C		
D		
E		
F		

Topic 17: Attention, please!

65 In diesem Bild werden einige neue Wörter erklärt. Lies jeden Satz sorgfältig. Entscheide jeweils, welche deutsche Bedeutung am besten passt.

> Mitarbeiter – Gleis/Bahnsteig – schwer – Fahrgäste – Fahrkarte – kostenlos

a) The people on a train are the **passengers**. _____

b) A train stops at a **platform** in a station. _____

c) 50 kilos is a **heavy** bag. _____

d) Forty people work at the station.
   These people are the **staff**. _____

e) The drink is **free**. It costs nothing. _____

f) You must buy a **ticket** to go on the train. _____

66 Sieh dir die Bilder in Aufgabe 67 genau an.
Kannst du erraten, worum es im Text gehen wird?
Beantworte die folgenden Fragen auf Deutsch.

a) In welcher Situation könnte man den Text hören?
   _____

b) Worum könnte es im Text gehen? Schreibe zwei Stichpunkte auf.
   • _____
   • _____

67 Höre die erste Durchsage an. Welches Bild beantwortet jeweils die Frage? Hake (✓) das richtige Kästchen ab – A, B oder C.

Track 8

> **Step up!**
> - Bei **Multiple Choice** Aufgaben mit Bildern solltest du vor dem Hören überlegen, welche Unterschiede es zwischen den Bildern gibt (z. B. verschiedene Uhrzeiten, Orte).
> - Beim Hören musst du dann besonders gut aufpassen, wenn z. B. von Zeitangaben oder Ortsnamen die Rede ist. ■

a) What time is the train to Manchester today?

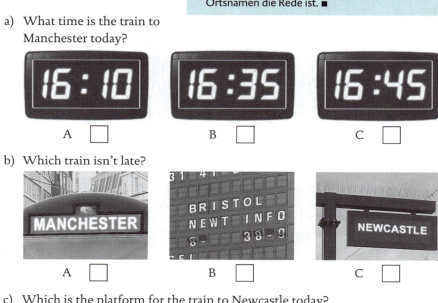

b) Which train isn't late?

c) Which is the platform for the train to Newcastle today?

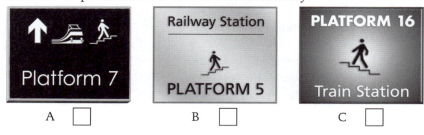

d) Who can get help?

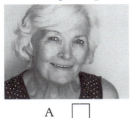

A ☐ B ☐ C ☐

68 Sieh dir die Bilder genau an. Höre dir dann die zweite Durchsage an.
Hake (✓) nur die Bilder in der Tabelle ab, die etwas mit dem Text zu tun haben.

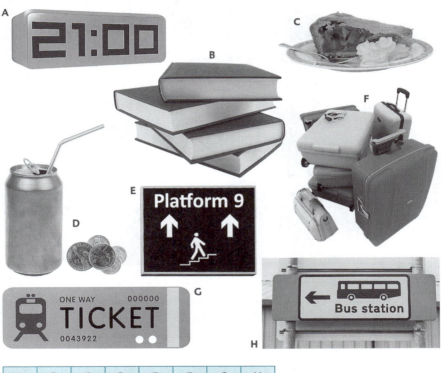

A	B	C	D	E	F	G	H

Topic 18: Crime Stop

69 Ordne jedem englischen Wort ein Bild und die passende Bedeutung zu.

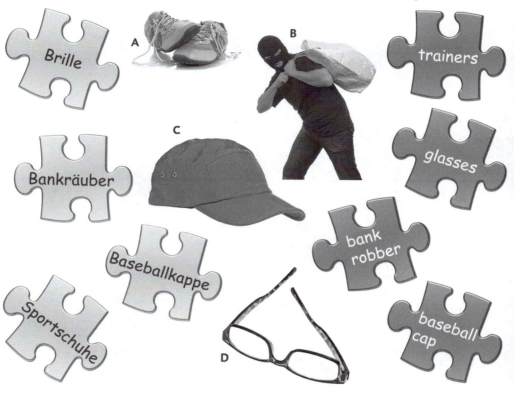

Englisch	bank robber	baseball cap	glasses	trainers
Bild				
Deutsch				

70 Vervollständige jeden Satz mit einem der neuen Wörter.
- The _____ is in the bank.
- Kim has got new _____ for school.
- Peter is wearing _____. Now he can see!
- Linda has got a _____ on her head.

71 „Crime Stop" ist eine Fernsehsendung, in der die Polizei die Zuschauer bei der Aufklärung von Verbrechen um Hilfe bittet. Höre dir an, was die Leute sagen. Welche Aussagen sind richtig *(true)* und welche sind falsch *(false)*? Hake (✓) die passenden Kästchen ab. Korrigiere falsche Aussagen.

	true	false
a) Crime Stop is looking for two bank robbers.	☐	☐
b) The man is 1.97 metres.	☐	☐
c) He is about 30 years old.	☐	☐
d) He has got blonde hair.	☐	☐
e) He is wearing a blue shirt and black trousers.	☐	☐
f) He has got a cap.	☐	☐
g) The second bank robber is 42 years old.	☐	☐
h) The second bank robber is a man.	☐	☐
i) There is a number on the T-shirt.	☐	☐
j) The number of the car is AWK 59 EB.	☐	☐
k) The telephone number is: 0961/ 3269.	☐	☐

72 Finde die zwei Bankräuber am Bahnhof. Schreibe den richtigen Buchstaben (a–h) auf.

- The first bank robber is: _____
- The second bank robber is: _____

Topic 19: Radio Boston

73 Welche Bilder passen zu diesen englischen Wörtern? Fülle die Tabelle aus.

> studio – umbrella – rain – sale – half price

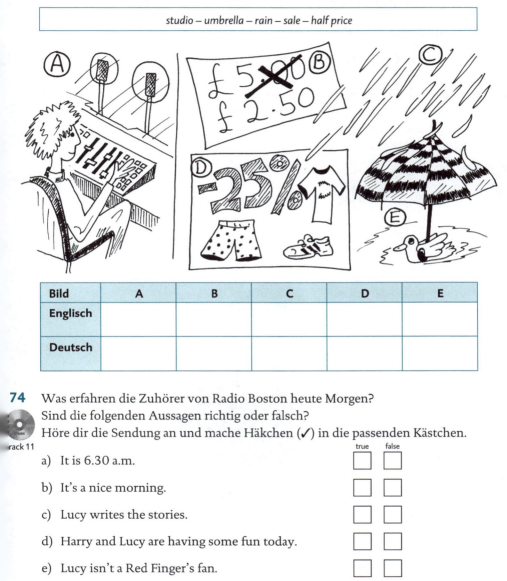

Bild	A	B	C	D	E
Englisch					
Deutsch					

74 Was erfahren die Zuhörer von Radio Boston heute Morgen?
Sind die folgenden Aussagen richtig oder falsch?
Höre dir die Sendung an und mache Häkchen (✓) in die passenden Kästchen.

                                                        true false

a) It is 6.30 a.m.

b) It's a nice morning.

c) Lucy writes the stories.

d) Harry and Lucy are having some fun today.

e) Lucy isn't a Red Finger's fan.

f) The internet price is $ 6.75.

g) Things are happening in Boston Common Park this afternoon. ☐ ☐

h) The MusicMan is in West Road. ☐ ☐

i) You can buy cheap CDs near Quincy Market today. ☐ ☐

j) The weather report (= *Wetterbericht*) is next. ☐ ☐

75 Heute Morgen war der Tontechniker Harry mit den Aufnahmen von Lucys Programm nicht zufrieden. Daher testete er den Ton an einigen Wörtern aus der Sendung. Welche wählte er aus?
Markiere alle Begriffe, die in der Sendung vorkamen.

- roads
- wet
- window
- download
- 2.15
- disco
- half price
- $ 7.50
- live music
- Hill Street

Topic 20: Answering questions

***76** Bei Aufgabe 77 wirst du sieben Fragen hören.
Du sollst dann die Rolle der Person spielen, die antworten muss.
Du kannst jeweils aus drei Antwortmöglichkeiten auswählen.
Lies dir nun als Vorbereitung die möglichen Antworten durch und überlege jeweils, wie eine passende Frage lauten könnte.

a) ☐ It's 3.15. _What time is it? (Uhrzeit)_
   ☐ It's £ 6.99. _____
   ☐ There are six. _____

b) ☐ After lunch – about 2 o'clock. _____
   ☐ Of course. What time? _____
   ☐ No, I'm sorry. I'm in London tomorrow. _____

c) ☐ In the summer holidays. _____
   ☐ We're watching television. _____
   ☐ Germany is nice. _____

d) ☐ I like Oxford. _____
   ☐ I'm sorry, I don't know. _____
   ☐ No, you must go by train. _____

e) ☐ It's 14 George Street. _____
   ☐ It's about £ 5.00, I think. _____
   ☐ 0934 / 20202 _____

f) ☐ Two people are waiting. _____
   ☐ There are three bus stops. _____
   ☐ It's Tim@aol.com. _____

g) ☐ My dog's name is Bruce. _____
   ☐ It's in America. _____
   ☐ I'm from Scotland. _____

77 Höre dir nun die Fragen an und hake (✓) das richtige Kästchen ab.

Tracks 12/13

a) ☐ It's 3.15.
☐ It's £ 6.99.
☐ There are six.

b) ☐ After lunch – about 2 o'clock.
☐ Of course. What time?
☐ No, I'm sorry. I'm in London tomorrow.

c) ☐ In the summer holidays.
☐ We're watching television.
☐ Germany is nice.

d) ☐ I like Oxford.
☐ I'm sorry, I don't know.
☐ No, you must go by train.

e) ☐ It's 14 George Street.
☐ It's about £ 5.00, I think.
☐ 0934 / 20202

f) ☐ Two people are waiting.
☐ There are three bus stops.
☐ It's Tim@aol.com.

g) ☐ My dog's name is Bruce.
☐ It's in America.
☐ I'm from Scotland.

> **Step up!**
> - Hier geht es darum, dass du erkennst, wie man in einer bestimmten Situation richtig reagiert.
> - Achte während des Hörens darauf, ob eine der Fragen, die du dir bei Aufgabe 76 überlegt hast, vorkommt. Achte besonders auf Fragewörter (z. B. *when, what, how*).
> - Wenn du die Aufgabe gelöst hast, höre dir die Lösung an (Track 13) und überprüfe deine Antworten. ∎

Topic 21: What do you say?

78 Höre dir das Gespräch an. Du hörst wieder nur eine Seite der Unterhaltung. Deine Aufgabe ist es, die Rolle der zweiten Person zu übernehmen.
Was sagst du? Markiere nach jeder Aussage auf der CD eine passende Reaktion.

CD: …
YOU:
- ☐ Yes, for my new school.
- ☐ No, I want a bag for my holidays.
- ☐ Do you have school bags?

CD: …
YOU:
- ☐ My books are big.
- ☐ £ 35.00! That's a lot of money.
- ☐ This big – like my old bag.

CD: …
YOU:
- ☐ I can paint it.
- ☐ Have you got more colours?
- ☐ Green or blue, please.

CD: …
YOU:
- ☐ Yes, that's what I want.
- ☐ That's a green bag.
- ☐ This is my bag.

> **Step up!**
> - Höre zuerst die CD an, damit du alle Fragen und Reaktionen der anderen Person kennst. So kannst du erraten, welche Rolle du im Gespräch hast.
> - Lies dir die Auswahlmöglichkeiten durch und überlege beim zweiten Hören, welche Reaktionen in den Dialog passen.
> - Höre dir den Text noch ein weiteres Mal an und überprüfe deine Auswahl.
> - Höre dir das komplette Gespräch (Track 15) an und vergleiche mit deinen Antworten. ■

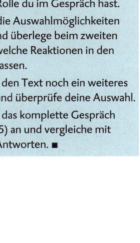

79 Höre dir das Gespräch an und übernimm wieder die Rolle der fehlenden Person. Wie lautet der vollständige Dialog?
Wähle die passenden Aussagen aus.

Tracks 16/17

CD: …
YOU:
- [ ] I want to go home.
- [ ] I think it's very nice, too.
- [ ] The café is nice.

CD: …
YOU:
- [ ] I don't like nice shops.
- [ ] Super, I want a book and some new clothes.
- [ ] When can we go to the museum?

CD: …
YOU:
- [ ] That's a good idea.
- [ ] We can go swimming.
- [ ] Where are the bikes?

CD: …
YOU:
- [ ] I want a new car.
- [ ] Yes, but not this week.
- [ ] No, it's only open today.

Topic 22: Kim's party

80 Was bedeuten diese Wörter auf Deutsch? Die Buchstaben, die du brauchst, um die deutschen Wörter zu bilden, stehen im Kasten.

(to) invite	__ __ __ l __ __ __ __
(to) book	__ __ c __ __ __
(to) stay	ü __ __ __ n __ __ __ __ __
possible	__ ö __ __ __ __ __
details	(hier) __ __ g __ b __ __
address	A __ __ __ __ __ __

```
n n e i d a l e
n e u b h c
r ü e b e c h n a n t
m g ö l i h c
n g e a A n b
A s e d e s r
```

81 Vervollständige die Lücken.
Verwende nur die neuen Vokabeln.

a) Here's my _____ – 14 Castle Street, Leeds.

b) I want to _____ in a nice hotel in New York.

c) Can I _____ Petra to our party?

d) Can you _____ a hotel room for me, please?

e) I want a large hotel room. Is that _____?

f) Can you give me your _____ for the hotel – your name, address and phone number?

82 Du hörst ein Telefongespräch über eine Party, allerdings hörst du nur, was Zoe sagt. Stelle dir vor, du bist Anne, die Person am anderen Ende der Leitung. Zoe hat dich angerufen. Was sagst du zu ihr?

Tracks 18/19

Wähle jeweils die Antwort aus, die am besten zum Gespräch passt.
Für jede Antwort hast du drei Wahlmöglichkeiten.
Die Lösung findest du ebenfalls auf der CD.

ZOE: *Hi Anne. . . .*

YOU: ☐ Is it her birthday?
☐ How old is she?
☐ Which sister?

ZOE: *No, ...*
YOU: ☐ That's terrible.
☐ What time is it?
☐ That's nice. –
  Where is it and what's she doing?

ZOE: *She's ...*
YOU: ☐ That's super. I want to go there, too.
☐ America? That's far away.
☐ Has she got a house there?

ZOE: *Me, ...*
YOU: ☐ What time is it?
☐ When is it?
☐ How big is the party?

ZOE: *It's ...*
YOU: ☐ Is the party at your house?
☐ That's a problem.
☐ That's OK. Where is the party?

ZOE: *It's ...*
YOU: ☐ Super. But we need a room for Friday and Saturday night in the hotel.
☐ Can we get breakfast in the hotel?
☐ Super. Is there a disco?

ZOE: *No ...*
YOU: ☐ That's great.
☐ What does she want?
☐ Why not?

ZOE: *Because ...*

83 Zoe telefoniert nun mit dem Red Cat Hotel, um die Übernachtung für Anne zu buchen.
Vervollständige das folgende Formular mit den Informationen aus dem Text.

Reservation form

Name(s): _____

Address: _____

Number of nights: _____

Date(s): _____

Arrive on: _____

Leave on: _____

Phone number: _____

Words and Spelling –
Strategien zum Kompetenzbereich Wortschatz und Rechtschreibung

Um eine Sprache gut zu beherrschen, ist es wichtig, einen möglichst umfangreichen Wortschatz zu haben. Dieses Kapitel vermittelt den Grundwortschatz zu bestimmten Themen, z. B. *school, animals* oder *family*.

- Am Anfang jedes *Topics* werden die neuen Vokabeln mithilfe der CD und oft mit Bildern eingeführt. Höre dir die CD so oft an, bis du dir eingeprägt hast, wie die Wörter ausgesprochen werden, und du deren Bedeutung sicher kennst. Im Anschluss daran findest du viele abwechslungsreiche Übungen, in denen du lernst, wie diese Wörter richtig verwendet werden. Mit jedem Kapitel wirst du so deinen Wortschatz erweitern.

- Die Übungen, in denen die neuen Vokabeln vorkommen, sind ganz unterschiedlich. Wenn du etwas nicht verstehen solltest, sieh im Lösungsteil nach. Aber vergiss nicht, die Aufgabe einige Wochen später noch einmal selbstständig zu machen.

- Es gibt unterschiedliche Verfahren, wie man Vokabeln lernen kann, z. B. mit dem Vokabelheft oder einem Karteikasten. Außerdem gibt es Tricks, wie man sich schwierige Wörter besser merken kann. In diesem Kapitel werden verschiedene Lerntechniken vorgestellt und geübt. Probiere sie aus und finde heraus, wie du am besten lernen kannst.

- Nur durch regelmäßiges Wiederholen kannst du dir Wörter dauerhaft merken. Das ist natürlich mühsam, lohnt sich aber. Neue Wörter musst du anfangs vielleicht täglich wiederholen bis du sie dir merken kannst. Nach ein bis zwei Wochen solltest du sie nochmals wiederholen. Mache dir einen Plan und lege fest, wann du welches Kapitel wiederholen möchtest.

- Nimm dir nicht zu viel auf einmal vor. Du wirst dir mehr merken können, wenn du jeden Tag zweimal 10 Minuten Vokabeln lernst, als wenn du an einem Tag eine ganze Stunde lernst und am nächsten gar nicht.

Topic 23: School and the classroom

84

Track 21

Höre dir die Wörter in der Liste an und lies dann die Sätze, in denen die Wörter verwendet werden. Schaue das Bild des Klassenzimmers an und beschrifte es mit den fünf Wörtern.

Step up!
- Sprich die Wörter, die du auf der CD hörst, laut nach und übe die richtige **Aussprache**.
- Am besten kannst du dies mit einem Partner üben. Vergleicht eure Aussprache gegenseitig mit der der Muttersprachler auf der CD. ■

> blackboard – chair – table – desk – notice board

The teacher writes on the **blackboard**.
We sit on **chairs**. We work on **tables**.
The teacher sits at a **desk** in the classroom.
School information is put on a **notice board** in the classroom.

Topic 23: School and the classroom 69

85 Dein Federmäppchen und sein Inhalt: Höre dir die englischen Wörter und die Erklärungen dazu an. Schreibe das richtige englische Wort in die Tabelle.

Tracks 22/23

Step up!
- Kannst du schon auf Englisch **buchstabieren**? Die Muttersprachler auf der CD helfen dir.
- In Track 22 kannst du dir das komplette Alphabet auf Englisch anhören. ■

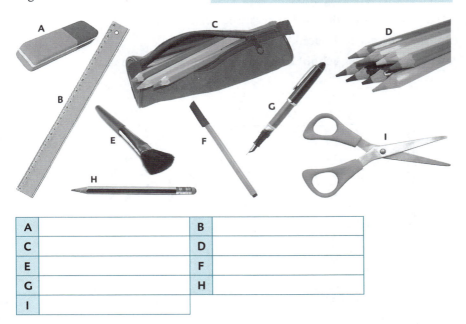

A		B	
C		D	
E		F	
G		H	
I			

86 Beschreibe, was Jenny in ihrem Federmäppchen hat und was fehlt.

Jenny has got _____
pencil crayons, _____
_____
_____
_____
and _____
But she hasn't got _____
_____
or _____

87 Vervollständige die Bilder zu den **fett** gedruckten englischen Wörtern. Wenn du die Sätze liest, solltest du erschließen können, was jedes Wort bedeutet. Schreibe das englische Wort unter jedes fertige Bild.

a) There is **a piece of paper** on the notice board.
b) Freddy has got a big **book**.
c) Lucy's **homework** is on her desk. She has three books to read.
d) Harry has got six **lessons** today at school.
e) Wendy has a big **school bag**. All her school books are in it.

Topic 24: House, home and garden

88 Höre dir die folgenden Wörter auf der CD an. Sieh dir dann das Bild an und schreibe die deutsche Bedeutung der Wörter auf.

a) chimney _____
b) door   _____
c) doorbell _____
d) doorstep _____
e) roof   _____
f) wall   _____
g) window   _____

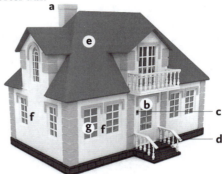

89 Sieh dir die Merkhilfen zu „chimney" und „doorstep" an. Überlege dir zu mindestens zwei der oben genannten neuen Wörter ein Bild als Merkhilfe. Schreibe die Wörter auf und zeichne das passende Bild dazu.

> **Step up!**
>
> Das kennst du bestimmt: Manche Wörter kann man sich einfach nicht merken, selbst wenn man sie ganz oft wiederholt.
> Es gibt verschiedene Möglichkeiten, wie du dir solche Wörter besser merken kannst:
>
> - Manchmal hilft es, wenn man sich Bilder als **Merkhilfen** dazu vorstellt. Stell dir bei *chimney* z. B. vor, dass aus dem „i" oder „h" kleine Rauchwölkchen kommen.
> - Bei anderen Wörtern erinnern Teile des Wortes an deutsche Wörter mit einer anderen Bedeutung (z. B. „*step*" in „*doorstep*" erinnert an „Stepptanz"). Du kannst dir hier als Merkhilfe vorstellen, wie jemand auf der Türschwelle steppt. ■

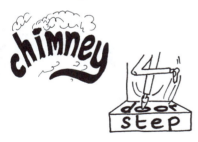

a) [   ]   b) [   ]

90 Nachdem er als Schiffbrüchiger auf einer einsamen Insel gelandet war, fing Max an, ein Haus zu bauen. Er fand viele Dinge, die er gebrauchen konnte.
Schreibe an die passenden Stellen, wofür jeder Gegenstand benutzt wurde.

91 Hier sind einige Verben, die man verwenden kann, wenn man über das Äußere eines Hauses spricht.
Versuche dich daran zu erinnern, welche Verben mit welchen Gegenständen gebraucht werden.
Track 25
Setze auch die entsprechende *ing*-Form der Verben ein.

a) (to) brush *(fegen)*	a window / a door	*brushing a doorstep*
b) (to) clean *(putzen)*	a doorstep	
c) (to) close *(schließen)*	a doorbell	
d) (to) open *(öffnen)*	a window	
e) (to) ring *(klingeln)*	a window / a door	

Topic 24: House, home and garden 73

92 Was tun die Leute auf dem Bild gerade?

a) Sam *is cleaning the window.*

b) Mrs Jones _____

c) Mandy _____

d) Kim _____

e) Fred _____

f) George _____

g) Rover _____

93 a) Höre dir folgende Wörter auf der CD an und präge dir die Bedeutung ein.
Sieh dir dann den Grundriss von Janets Haus an.
Schreibe die Namen der Zimmer auf den Grundriss.

downstairs	unten	upstairs	oben
dining room	Esszimmer	bathroom	Badezimmer
hall	Diele	bedroom	Schlafzimmer
kitchen	Küche	landing	Treppenabsatz
living room	Wohnzimmer	toilet	Toilette
stairs	Treppe		

b) Zeichne einen Grundriss deines Zuhauses und benenne die Teile, deren englische Bezeichnungen du kennst.

94 Die Namen folgender Gegenstände sind auf der CD. Sie werden gesprochen und buchstabiert. Schreibe jedes Wort neben das dazugehörige Bild.

a) _____

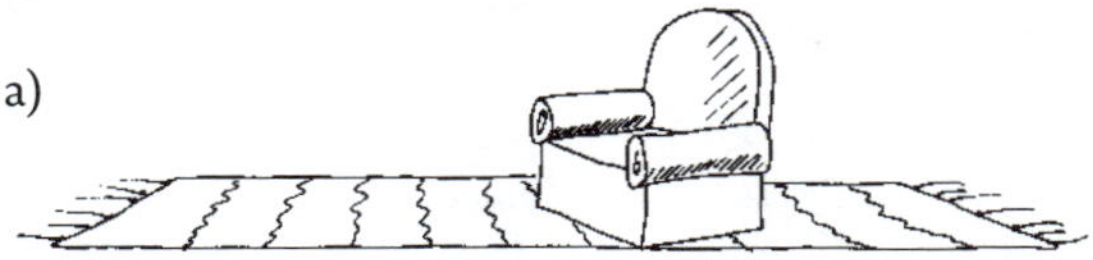

b) _____

c) _____

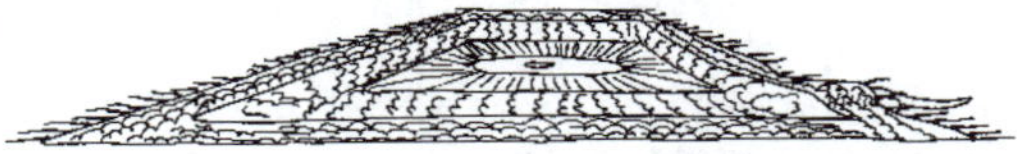

d) _____

e) _____

f) _____

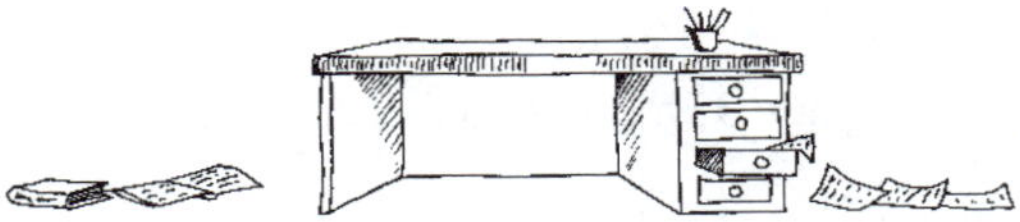

g) _____

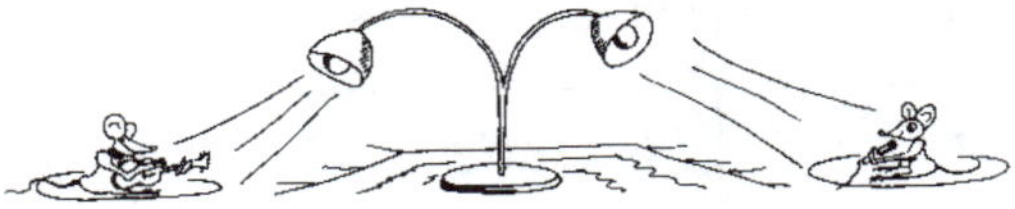

h) _____

i)  (pl.) _____

j) _____

k) _____

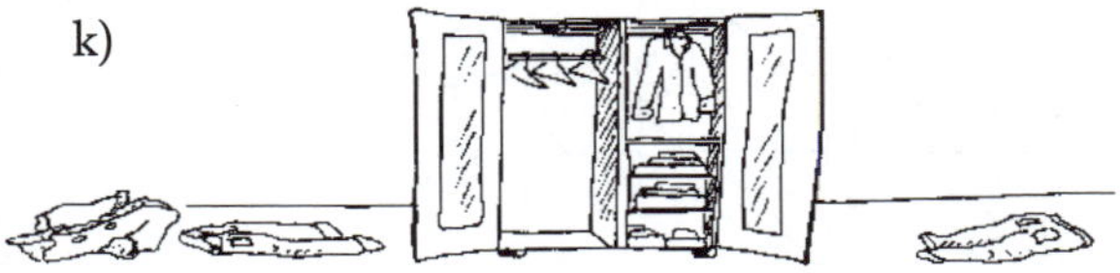

95 a) Familie Smith ist gerade in ihr neues Haus eingezogen, aber die Männer der Umzugsfirma haben viele Sachen in die falschen Zimmer gestellt.
Höre dir auf der CD an, wo die Gegenstände jetzt sind und wo sie eigentlich hingehören.
Vervollständige die Tabelle.

> **Step up!**
> - Höre dir den Text einmal komplett an, damit du ungefähr weißt, worum es geht.
> - Achte beim zweiten Hören darauf, wann von *Grandma, James* usw. die Rede ist und fülle die Tabelle aus.
> - Wenn nötig, kannst du dir den Text noch einmal anhören und deine Antworten überprüfen. ■

name	object	wrong room (✗)	right room (✓)
Grandma	armchair	bathroom	her room
James			
Karen			
George			
Mr Smith			
Mr & Mrs Smith			

b) Zeichne die Gegenstände aus Aufgabe 95 a in die richtigen Zimmer auf dem Grundriss ein.
Die genaue Position der Gegenstände in den Zimmern ist nicht so wichtig.

Topic 24: House, home and garden 77

96 Hier sind einige Wörter rund um das Thema „Garten".
Höre dir auf der CD an, wie sie ausgesprochen werden.
Schreibe die deutsche Bedeutung auf.

a) bush _____

b) flower _____

c) grass _____

d) hedge _____

e) pond _____

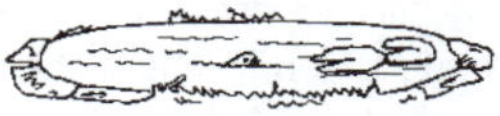

f) tree _____

g) drive _____

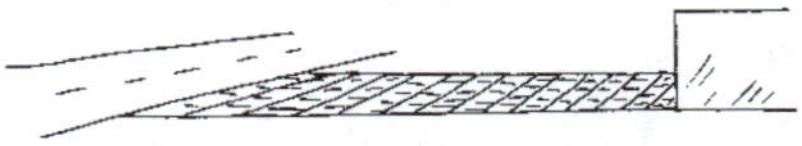

h) fence _____

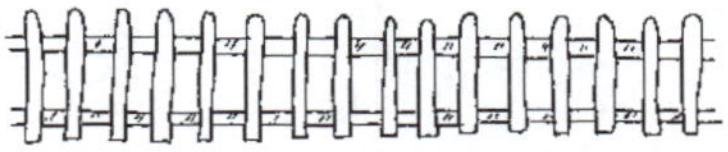

i) garage _____

j) gate _____

k) path _____

l) shed _____

Step up!

Wie lernst du Vokabeln? Eine Möglichkeit ist die **Vokabelkartei**.

- Du benötigst einen Karteikasten, der in verschiedene Bereiche unterteilt wird. Der erste Bereich ist am kleinsten, die folgenden werden immer größer.
- Schreibe die neuen Wörter auf Karteikarten. In Übung 97 siehst du, wie man das machen kann. Es liegt bei dir, wie viele Informationen du aufnehmen möchtest.
- Neue Vokabeln kommen immer in den vordersten Bereich deines Karteikastens und werden täglich wiederholt. Beim Lernen kannst du unterschiedlich vorgehen: Drehe bei allen Karten die deutsche Seite nach oben und sage die englische Bedeutung sowie einen Beispielsatz, wenn du die Karte herausnimmst. Oder gehe umgekehrt vor und übe die deutsche Bedeutung.
- Wenn du die Bedeutung gewusst hast, darfst du das Kärtchen ins nächste Fach einsortieren. Die Wörter, die du noch nicht so gut konntest, bleiben im ersten Fach. Die Wörter des zweiten Fachs wiederholst du nach ca. drei Tagen. Wenn du sie dann noch weißt, kommen sie wieder ein Fach nach hinten, wenn nicht, sortierst du sie wieder ins erste Fach ein. Auch die Wörter im dritten Fach wiederholst du nach einer Woche und gehst genauso vor. Die regelmäßige Wiederholung sorgt dafür, dass der Wortschatz wirklich sitzt.

Folgendes Schema fasst zusammen, wie die Arbeit mit der Kartei funktioniert:

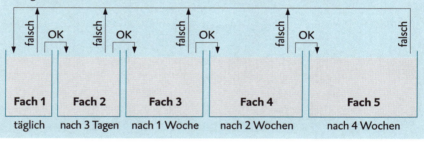

97 So könnte die Vorderseite einer Karteikarte aussehen. Überlege dir immer einen Beispielsatz. Schreibe auch Wörter auf, die man oft gemeinsam verwendet, z. B. das Nomen „tree" und das passende Verb „to climb a tree". Bei Nomen solltest du die Pluralform dazu schreiben. Auch die Aussprache kannst du hier notieren. Wenn möglich, zeichne ein Bild dazu und überlege dir eine Merkhilfe (vgl. Aufgabe 89). Fertige nun die Rückseite der Karteikarte mit den deutschen Wörtern bzw. Sätzen an.

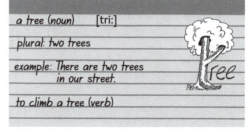

Beispiel für eine Vokabelkarteikarte

98 Suche dir nun zwei Wörter aus Aufgabe 96 aus und erstelle Karteikarten nach diesem Beispiel.

a)

> **Step up!**
> Du kannst deine Kartei ganz unterschiedlich sortieren:
> - Wenn du z. B. das Thema „Garten" behandelst, sammle alle Wörter, die dazu passen in einem Fach und übe sie besonders häufig. ■

b)

99 Wer wohnt wo? Sieh dir die Zeichnung genau an und lies die Geschichte sorgfältig. Finde heraus, wer in welchem Haus wohnt.

Jenny has got two trees in her garden. Mike has got a pond in his garden. Jane's pond is next to (= *neben*) her shed. Bob's garden has got a white fence and a lot of (= *viele*) trees. The garden next to Jenny's is Anne's. Anne's garden has got a hedge and a path to her shed. Peter hasn't got grass in his garden. Mary has got a lot of flowers in her garden and a bush next to her pond. James has got a long drive and a big garage.

House	1	2	3	4	5	6	7	8
Name								

100 Lies folgende Sätze und zeichne ein, wo sich die Dinge befinden. Statt zu zeichnen kannst du auch die Buchstaben a–f eintragen.

a) The book is in the pond.
b) The pen is on the path.
c) The bag is in the bush.
d) The ball is on the drive. It's under the car.
e) The radio is on the grass next to the tree.
f) The skateboard is in front of the shed.

Topic 25: Colours

01 Lerne alle diese Farben, die du auf der CD hörst.

black	–	schwarz	blue	–	blau	brown	–	braun
green	–	grün	grey	–	grau	orange	–	orange
purple	–	lila	red	–	rot	white	–	weiß
yellow	–	gelb						

Step up!

Eine weitere Möglichkeit, Vokabeln zu lernen ist das **Vokabelheft**. Am besten verwendest du ein großes Heft, in dem du jede Seite in **drei Spalten** einteilst.

- Schreibe in die erste Spalte das englische Wort und in die dritte das deutsche Wort.
- Überlege dir einen Beispielsatz und schreibe ihn in die mittlere Spalte. Hier kannst du zusätzlich alles aufschreiben oder zeichnen, was dir hilft, dir das Wort zu merken: z. B. ein Wort, das das Gegenteil (*opposite*) oder fast das Gleiche (*synonym*) bedeutet, ein Bild oder eine Merkhilfe (vgl. Aufgabe 89).
- Decke beim Lernen abwechselnd die englische und die deutsche Seite mit einem Blatt ab und schreibe die Bedeutung auf, die verdeckt ist. Wenn du gerade die englische Spalte und die Mittelspalte abgedeckt hast, sage (und schreibe) auch einen Beispielsatz.
- Überlege dir eine Markierung für Wörter, die du noch nicht so gut kannst. Markiere mit Symbolen oder unterschiedlichen Farben, ob Aussprache (z. B. Symbol Mund), Schreibung (z. B. Stift) oder Bedeutung (z. B. !) schwierig zu merken sind. Konzentriere dich beim nächsten Durchgang auf diese Wörter. ■

| blue | I like the colour blue very much. | blau |

Beispiel für ein dreispaltiges Vokabelheft

02 Male die Wörter in der richtigen Farbe aus. Zeichne zu jeder Farbe einen Gegenstand oder ein Tier, den bzw. das du mit dieser Farbe verbindest (z. B. einen Esel zur Farbe Grau), in dein Vokabelheft oder auf deine Karteikarten.

Words and Spelling

103 König Richard hat seinen Schatz vor seinem bösen Bruder John am Fuß einer Geheimtreppe versteckt. Prinz John konnte ihn nicht finden.
Kannst du den Schatz aufspüren? Beantworte die Fragen der Reihe nach und schreibe die Farben auf die Treppe. Jede Stufe enthält nur einen Buchstaben.
Du musst die letzte Stufe erreichen, um den Schatz zu finden.

a) What colour is grass *(Gras)*?   _green_
b) What colour is the sun *(Sonne)*?   _____
c) What colour is a tomato *(Tomate)*?   _____
d) What three colours are traffic lights *(Ampel)*?   _____
e) What colour is wood *(Holz)*?   _____
f) What colour is the sky *(Himmel)* at night?   _____
g) What colour is a polar bear *(Eisbär)*?   _____
h) What colour is a plum *(Pflaume)*?   _____
i) What colour is the sky on a sunny day *(sonnigen Tag)*?   _____

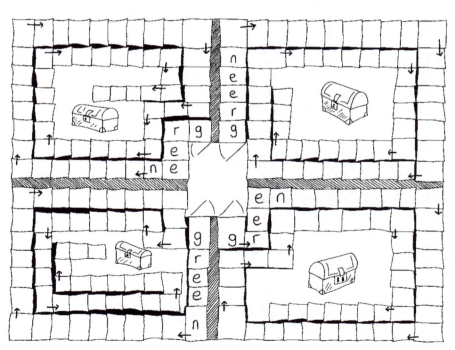

04 Lass uns ein Bild zusammen malen. Die Buntstifte, die du brauchst, sind: blau, gelb, grau, lila, orange, rot und schwarz. Während du die CD anhörst, kannst du die Gegenstände mit den passenden Buntstiften markieren. Wenn die CD zu Ende ist, kannst du das Bild dann besser malen. Höre die Anweisungen auf der CD an. Beachte: Die Gegenstände hier haben nicht ihre normale Farbe.

Topic 26: The family

105 Höre dir die Wörter zum Thema Familie an und lerne sie.

Track 32

aunt	–	Tante
brother	–	Bruder
cousin	–	Cousine / Cousin
daughter	–	Tochter
dad	–	Papa / Vati
(father)		(Vater)
grandad	–	Opa
(grandfather)		(Großvater)
grandma	–	Oma
(grandmother)		(Großmutter)
mum	–	Mama / Mutti
(mother)		(Mutter)
sister	–	Schwester
son	–	Sohn
uncle	–	Onkel

Step up!

Beachte: Wenn *mum* oder *dad* statt eines Namens verwendet werden, werden sie großgeschrieben, sonst schreibt man sie klein.

Beispiele:
- I am helping <u>Dad</u> wash his car.
  (In diesem Fall könnte *Dad* durch einen Namen, z. B. John, ersetzt werden.)
- I am helping <u>my</u> <u>mum</u> wash her car.
  (Hier kann man *mum* nicht durch einen Namen ersetzen.)

Wenn *aunt* oder *uncle* allein verwendet werden, werden sie kleingeschrieben. Stehen sie vor einem Namen, z. B. *Aunt Jane*, so schreibt man sie groß.

Beispiele:
- I am visiting my <u>aunt</u>.
- I am visiting <u>Uncle Steve</u>. ∎

106 Schreibe deinen Stammbaum auf und beschrifte ihn auf Englisch mit den neuen Wörtern.

07 Hier ist Lucys Stammbaum. Schreibe in den folgenden Sätzen die Verwandtschaftsverhältnisse der Familienmitglieder auf.

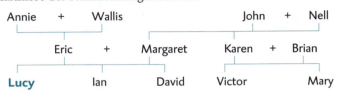

a) Ian is David's _____

b) Mary is David's _____

c) Lucy is David's _____

d) Eric is Ian's _____

e) Annie is Lucy's _____

f) Nell is Margaret's _____

g) John is Ian's _____

h) Karen is David's _____

i) Brian is Lucy's _____

j) Annie is Eric's _____

08 Versuche, die folgenden Rätsel mithilfe von Lucys Stammbaum zu lösen. Schreibe jeweils den Namen auf und wie die Person mit Lucy verwandt ist.
Beispiel: Who is Ian's mother's mother?
   Nell / _grandmother_

a) Who is Lucy's aunt's daughter?   _____ / _____

b) Who are Wallis's son's sons?   _____ / _____

c) Who is Victor's mother's father?   _____ / _____

09 Diktat: Höre dir die Sätze an und fülle die Lücken aus. Überlege genau, ob die Wörter groß oder klein geschrieben werden. Hier fehlen außerdem die Satzzeichen. Höre genau zu und trage die richtigen Satzzeichen ein.

| Komma | – | *comma* | Punkt | – | *full stop* |
| Fragezeichen | – | *question mark* | Ausrufezeichen | – | *exclamation mark* |

a) Mick and John are visiting _____
   _____
   but Kim is watching TV with _____
   _____

b) SAM: _____
   _____ today
   MUM: Yes I am I'm giving _____
   _____

c) JACKIE: _____ where's _____
   DAD: She's in the garden She's talking to
   _____

d) MR SMITH: Karen is _____
   KAREN: No he isn't But _____
   MR SMITH: Can I speak to _____

> **Step up!**
> - Bei einem **Diktat** ist der Text immer zweimal auf der CD. Zuerst wird er komplett vorgelesen, damit du weißt, worum es geht. Höre dir den Text zuerst nur an und schreibe noch nicht mit. Beim zweiten Vorlesen werden Pausen gemacht, damit du mitschreiben kannst.
> - Sollte es dir dennoch zu schnell gehen, drücke während des Diktats auf „Pause".
> - Zur Übung kannst du dir den Text ruhig mehrmals anhören. ■

110 Hier sind noch weitere Wörter zum Thema Familie. Höre dir die CD an und lerne sie. Einige davon kannst du diesem Familienfoto zuordnen. Schreibe sie an die passende(n) Stelle(n).

Track 34

baby	–	*Baby*	child (children)	–	*Kind (Kinder)*
grandparents	–	*Großeltern*	husband	–	*Ehemann*
nephew	–	*Neffe*	niece	–	*Nichte*
parents	–	*Eltern*	wife	–	*Ehefrau*

111 Diktat: Tom und Jo haben heute Gäste zum Abendessen.

a) Höre dir das Gespräch zwischen Tom und Jo an und ergänze die fehlenden Wörter.

JO: Where are people sitting, Tom?

TOM: I don't know. Can you help me?

JO: Of course. Abi's _____ can sit next to *(neben)* her.
Her _____ can sit on Abi's left and her _____
_____ on her right.

TOM: Abi's _____ can sit next to her _____
and her _____ next to her _____.

JO: Put John, her _____, next to Abi's _____
and Karen, John's _____, next to Abi's _____.
We can then put Abi's _____, _____
and her _____, George, on the last three seats.
George goes between his _____.
Put Abi's _____ on George's right, next to John.

TOM: Haven't John and Karen got any children?

JO: Yes, they have, a boy and a girl. But Abi's _____ and
_____ can't come to the party.

b) Sieh dir nun den Esstisch an und schreibe die Sitzordnung an die dafür vorgesehenen Stellen.

112 Wie lautet das englische Wort für „Verwandte (pl.)"?
Vervollständige das Rätsel auf Englisch und du hast die Antwort.

Großeltern
Tochter
Kind
Vati / Papa
Bruder
Cousine
Sohn
Ehemann
Schwester

113 Hier sind einige Wörter, mit denen man Menschen beschreiben kann.
Ordne jedem von ihnen das passende deutsche Wort zu.
Schreibe die Bildnummer und das deutsche Wort an die richtige Stelle.
Track 36   Sieh genau hin, denn dir werden einige Anhaltspunkte gegeben.

friendly	funny	nice	old	pretty	small	tall	young
e							
freund-lich							

Topic 26: The family 89

114 Sieh dir die folgenden Zeichnungen an und beschreibe jede Person mit einem der neuen Wörter, die du gerade gelernt hast.

a) Robert's grandfather is _old_.

b) Jenny's aunt is _____.

c) Kevin's uncle is _____.

d) William's brother is _____.

e) Jenny is _____.

f) Roberta's sister is very _____.

g) Norman's father is _____.

Topic 27: Clothes

115 Höre dir die englischen Bezeichnungen für folgende Kleidungsstücke an. Wie heißen sie auf Deutsch?

Track 37

a) blouse

b) dress

c) (a pair of) jeans

d) pullover

e) shirt

f) (a pair of) shorts

g) skirt

h) (a pair of) socks

i) sweatshirt

j) tie

k) (a pair of) trousers

l) T-shirt

Step up!

Bei einigen Kleidungsstücken wird im Englischen „*a pair of*" verwendet. Versuche, die folgenden Ausdrücke zu lernen:

<u>*a pair of*</u> *trousers / jeans / shorts / socks / gloves / shoes* (+ alle Arten von Schuhen) ∎

116 Alle Mitglieder der Familie Peters haben neue Kleidungsstücke gekauft.
Sieh dir die Zeichnungen genau an und schreibe, was jeder von ihnen Neues trägt. Denke daran, wo nötig „*a pair of*" zu benutzen.

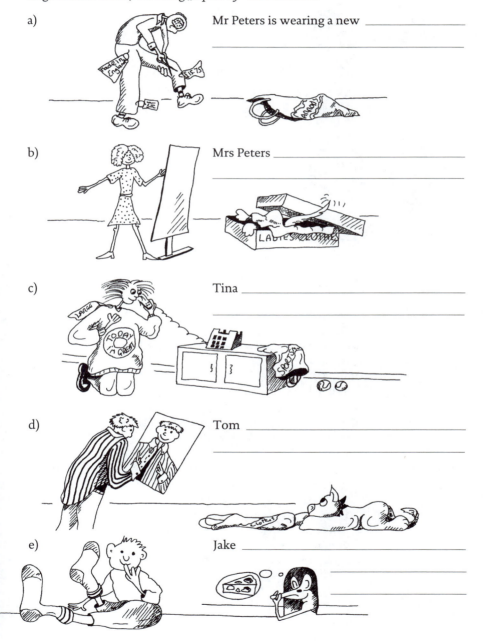

a) Mr Peters is wearing a new _____

b) Mrs Peters _____

c) Tina _____

d) Tom _____

e) Jake _____

117 Für draußen brauchst du je nach Wetter besondere Kleidung.
Höre dir die CD an und schreibe die Namen für jedes Kleidungsstück auf.

Track 38

A	B	C	D	E	F
				pl.:	

118 Welche Wörter in diesem Kapitel sind besonders schwer für dich? Probiere die Methoden aus, die in „Step up!" vorgestellt werden.

Step up!

Nicht jeder Mensch lernt auf die gleiche Weise. Für manche ist es besonders wichtig, etwas zu sehen, für andere ist Hören wichtiger oder selbst etwas zu tun.
Probiere verschiedene Techniken aus, um herauszufinden, welcher **Lerntyp** du bist.

- **Sehen/tun:** Schreibe die Wörter, die du dir nicht gut merken kannst auf Karten und hänge sie in deinem Zimmer auf, die Wörter zu *clothes* z. B. an die Fächer deines Kleiderschrankes. Wenn du also Socken aus dem Fach nimmst, siehst du immer das passende englische Wort dazu. Zeichne außerdem ein Bild zu den Wörtern und überlege dir eine Merkhilfe (vgl. Aufgabe 89).
- **Hören/sprechen:** Sage die Wörter laut vor dich hin. Überlege dir einen bestimmten Rhythmus oder lies sie mit übertriebener Betonung vor. Sage die Wörter auf besondere Art: z. B. laut, geflüstert, schnell, langsam oder mit verstellter Stimme. Du kannst diese Übungen auch aufnehmen und immer wieder anhören. ∎

Topic 27: Clothes 93

19 Diktat: Hannah und ihr Bruder Lewis fahren jedes Jahr gemeinsam in Urlaub. Sie wohnen immer im selben Hotel am Meer. Was packt jeder von ihnen ein? Höre dir die Texte an und schreibe mit.

> **Step up!**
> In diesen Diktaten kommen neben den Vokabeln zum Thema Kleidung auch viele **Zahlen** vor.
> - Schreibe Zahlen bis zwölf als Wort (*one, two, three, four, …*).
> - Wenn du hier unsicher bist, sieh dir die Zahlen noch einmal in deinem Schulbuch an. ∎

a) Lewis: _____

_____

_____

_____

_____

_____

b) Hannah: _____

_____

_____

_____

_____

_____

20 Schreibe ein oder zwei Sätze über die folgenden Dinge. Verwende die Wörter, die du in diesem Kapitel gelernt hast.

a) Beschreibe, was du gerade trägst.

_____

_____

b) Es schneit. Du gehst nach draußen. Was ziehst du an?

_____

_____

121 Die Tiere vom Zoo von Winchester haben den Besuchern Kleidungsstücke gestohlen. Welches Tier hat was?

a) The monkey has got _____

b) The lion _____

c) The bear _____

d) The kangaroo _____

e) The elephant _____

f) The seal _____

Topic 28: Animals and pets

122 Du hörst auf der CD eine Reihe von Tiernamen.
Schreibe jeden Tiernamen zum passenden Bild.

a) _____

b) _____

c) _____

d) _____

e) _____

f) _____

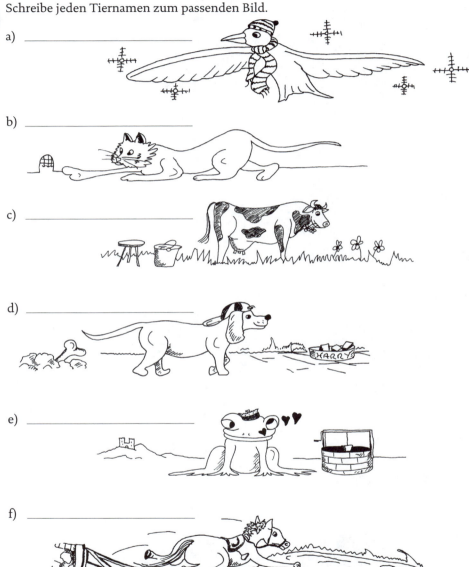

Words and Spelling

g) _____

h) _____

i) _____

123 Sieh dir die Zeichnung genau an und fülle die Lücken in den Sätzen auf der nächsten Seite aus.

Topic 28: Animals and pets   97

a) Noel _is feeding_ (füttern) a big _____.

b) Julie _____ (gehen) to her _____.

c) Michael _____ (schwimmen) with the _____.

d) Tina _is looking for_ (suchen) the _____.

e) George _is milking_ (melken) a _____.

f) James _____ (tragen) a bag with a _____ on it.

g) Linda _____ (laufen) with her _____.

h) Chris _____ (tragen) a _____ mask.

i) Vicky _____ (spielen) with her _____.

24 a) Sieh dir die Bilder an und entscheide, welche Tiere du für das Wörterrätsel brauchst. Suche die englische und die deutsche Bedeutung im Rätsel und setze beide Wörter an der passenden Stelle ein.

E	S	B	I	R	D	F
M	O	U	S	E	F	V
A	B	S	R	D	R	O
U	F	C	C	D	O	G
S	R	H	O	R	S	E
H	O	A	W	A	C	L
U	G	F	K	U	H	C
N	P	F	E	R	D	A
D	K	A	T	Z	E	T
S	H	E	E	P	R	A

b) Weißt du, wie diese Tiere heißen, wenn sie noch ganz jung sind?
Die Buchstaben in deinen Antworten zu Übung 124 a sind nummeriert.
Ersetze die Nummern in den Antwortkästchen hier durch die entsprechenden Buchstaben aus Übung 124 a und du findest die Antwort.

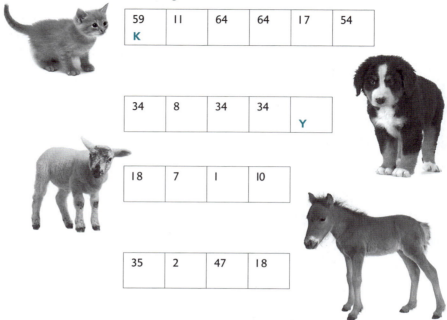

59	11	64	64	17	54
K					

34	8	34	34
			Y

18	7	1	10

35	2	47	18

125 Es macht Spaß Comicfiguren zu zeichnen. Kannst du für eines der Tiere eine Comicfigur zeichnen und ihr einen englischen Namen geben, der mit demselben Buchstaben beginnt wie das Tier? So merkst du dir die Tiernamen ganz bestimmt! *Beispiel*: **P**ercy the **P**ig.

Topic 29: The body

26 Du hörst auf der CD die englischen Bezeichnungen für Körperteile. Kannst du die deutschen Wörter ergänzen?

Track 42

a) arm

b) back

c) chest

d) foot (pl. feet)

e) finger

f) hand

g) head

h) knee

i) leg

j) neck

k) thumb

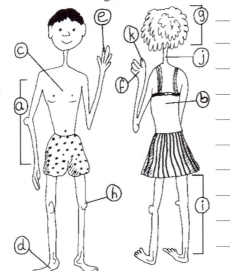

27 Manchmal stimmt etwas mit deinem Körper nicht und tut weh. Du hörst auf der CD einige Wörter, die beschreiben, was nicht stimmt. Achte besonders auf die Ausdrücke, bei denen „a" verwendet wird.

broken	*(gebrochen)*	I have got <u>a broken leg</u>.
cold	*(Schnupfen, Erkältung)*	She has got <u>a cold</u>.
headache	*(Kopfschmerzen)*	He has got <u>a headache</u>.
(to) hurt	*(verletzen, wehtun)*	Her arm <u>hurts</u>.
(to) feel ill	*(sich krank fühlen)*	Andrew <u>feels ill</u>.
sore	*(entzündet/schmerzhaft)*	Mary has got <u>a sore</u> finger.
swollen	*(geschwollen)*	Peter has got <u>a swollen</u> arm.
toothache	*(Zahnschmerzen)*	Mrs Smith has got <u>toothache</u>.

Step up!
- Überlege dir zu diesen Wörtern wieder Bilder, die dir helfen, die Wörter zu behalten.
- Manche Schüler können sich Wörter gut merken, wenn sie sie hören. Wenn es dir genauso geht, übe besonders häufig mit der CD. Wenn du einmal keine CD-Aufnahme hast, nimm die Wörter selbst auf (z. B. mit deinem Handy oder einem Diktiergerät). Überlege dir auch immer einen Beispielsatz. ■

128 Sieh dir die Zeichnungen sorgfältig an und schreibe auf, was diesen Menschen fehlt.

a) Jenny has got a _____

b) Mike's hand _____

c) Peter has got a _____

d) Mandy's got _____

e) Robert has got a _____

f) Georgina has got a _____

g) Ken has got a _____

Topic 29: The body | 101

29 In der Praxis der Ärztin ist heute viel zu tun.
Höre dir den Dialog auf der CD an und mache eine Terminliste.
Achte auf die richtige zeitliche Reihenfolge. Nicht jede Zeile wird benötigt.
Schreibe auch auf, was jedem Patienten fehlt.

time	name	illness (Krankheit)
2.30		
2.45		
3.00		
3.15		
3.30		
3.45		
4.00		
4.15		

30 Diktat: Heute kommen noch weitere Patienten zu der Ärztin.
Höre dir die Dialoge an und schreibe mit.

MR LONDON: Hello, my name is Peter London. _____
_____

RECEPTIONIST: Of course, please sit over there.
MISS RICHARDS: _____
_____
_____

RECEPTIONIST: Wait over there, please.
MRS BIRD: _____
_____
_____
_____

RECEPTIONIST: _____
_____
_____

131 Lege ein Vokabelnetz für das Wortfeld „*the body*" an. Als Hilfe sind hier schon einige Äste eingezeichnet. Du kannst dir aber auch eine andere Gliederung überlegen und das Netz auf ein Blatt schreiben/zeichnen.

Step up!
Wenn du dir die Wörter eines ganzen Wortfeldes merken musst, hilft es, wenn du ein **Vokabelnetz** aufzeichnest. Hier werden die Wörter sinnvoll angeordnet und Beziehungen zwischen Wörtern eingezeichnet.
- Nimm ein großes Blatt (DIN A 3) und schreibe das Thema in die Mitte, z. B. *the body*. Überlege, wie du die Wörter gliedern kannst und zeichne Äste zu den Oberbegriffen (z. B. *parts of the body*, *illnesses*). Zeichne davon aus weitere Äste und schreibe die Wörter dazu. Wichtig ist, dass du dir selbst eine Gliederung überlegst, denn dabei prägst du dir die Wörter ein.
- Zeichne, wo möglich, ein kleines Bild zu den Wörtern. ∎

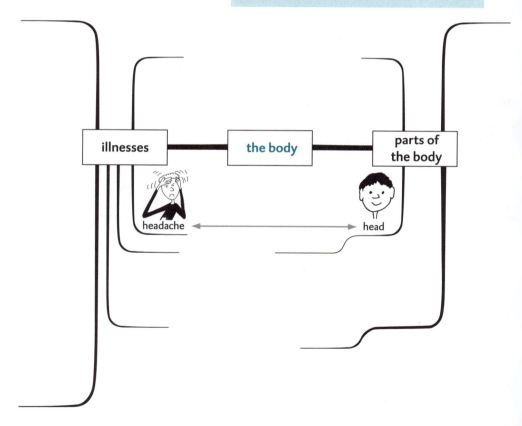

Topic 30: British or American English?

32 a) Höre dir an, was die Amerikanerin Jessica, die Engländerin Rachel und Markus aus Deutschland über britisches und amerikanisches Englisch sagen. Sechs Wörter, über die sie sprechen, sind: *sidewalk, cell phone, fries, pavement, mobile* und *chips*.

German	American English	British English
Handy		

b) Im zweiten Teil des Gesprächs werden die Wörter buchstabiert. Passe gut auf und fülle die Tabelle aus. Einige deutsche Wörter sind nicht im Dialog enthalten, aber du solltest sie kennen.

German	American English	British English
		colour

133 Wenn du schreibst, darfst du britische und amerikanische Schreibung nicht vermischen. Schreibe die folgenden Sätze richtig: Schreibe jeden Satz einmal in amerikanischem Englisch, einmal in britischem Englisch. Wenn du denkst, dass ein Satz schon richtig (d. h. entweder in amerikanischem oder britischem Englisch) ist, schreibe ihn nur auf die andere Art.

a) He walks along the sidewalk talking to his friend on his mobile.

b) "I like the colour of your neighbor's car," says Julie.

c) The pavement in the town center is new.

d) The café next to the jewelry shop sells great fries.

e) Can I use your cell phone to phone my friend at the harbour, please?

134 Sieh dir die Schilder auf der nächsten Seite an.
Welche Schilder sind aus Amerika und welche Schilder sind aus England?
Fülle die Tabelle aus und schreibe den Ausdruck auf, der dir bei deiner Entscheidung hilft.

Topic 30: British or American English?

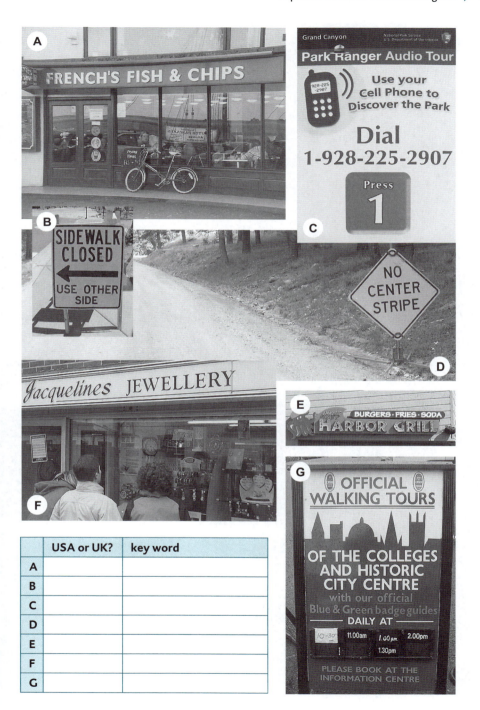

	USA or UK?	key word
A		
B		
C		
D		
E		
F		
G		

Mediation –
Strategien zum Kompetenzbereich Sprachmittlung

In einer Mediation, die man auch Sprachmittlung nennt, erhältst du einen Text, ein Schild oder ähnliche Materialien auf Englisch oder Deutsch. Deine Aufgabe ist es, den Inhalt zu verstehen und wichtige Informationen in die jeweils andere Sprache zu übertragen. Dabei ist immer eine Situation vorgegeben, in der du einer anderen Person den Inhalt vermitteln sollst, weil diese Englisch bzw. Deutsch nicht versteht. Solche Situationen können ganz unterschiedlich aussehen: Du musst z. B. Schilder oder Durchsagen erklären, Fragen zu Lesetexten beantworten oder zwischen verschiedenen Personen dolmetschen.
Schwierigere Aufgaben sind wieder mit einem Sternchen (*) gekennzeichnet.

- Du darfst Mediation nicht mit Übersetzung verwechseln. Es geht nicht darum, einen Text wortwörtlich zu übersetzen. Stattdessen sollst du die gegebenen Informationen in eine andere Sprache übertragen. Verwende dabei die Wörter, die du bis jetzt schon gelernt hast, um Informationen zu umschreiben.

- Bei einigen Aufgaben kommen Hörverstehenstexte vor. Ausführliche Tipps dazu findest du auch im Kapitel *Listening*. Neben einigen Aufgaben sind außerdem weitere Tipps angegeben („Step up!"), wie du Mediationsaufgaben am besten meistern kannst.

Topic 31: A visit to Norfolk

135 a)

Step up!
- Es wird immer wieder vorkommen, dass einige **Wörter** für dich **unbekannt** sind. Das ist ganz normal. Vieles kannst du aus dem Zusammenhang ableiten. Die Wörter in „*Caution: uneven surface*" (= Vorsicht, unebene Oberfläche) sind sicher neu für dich. Wenn du die Aufgabe liest, merkst du aber, dass danach nicht gefragt wird.
- Lies also immer zuerst die Aufgabe und suche dann gezielt nach Informationen dazu auf dem Schild.
- Vergleiche bei **Multiple Choice** Aufgaben die Auswahlmöglichkeiten sorgfältig mit dem Schild. Oft sind sich die Auswahlmöglichkeiten sehr ähnlich. ■

Du bist mit deiner Familie in Norfolk, Ostengland.
Ihr seid gerade mit dem Auto bei einem Park angekommen und seht dieses Schild.
Dein kleiner Bruder kann noch nicht so gut Englisch. Er möchte wissen, was das Schild bedeutet.
Wähle die beste Antwort aus und mache ein Häkchen (✓).

☐ Ihr müsst weiterfahren, weil man nicht auf dem Gras parken darf. Hunde müssen an die Leine.

☐ Autos sollen auf dem Gras geparkt werden. Der Ausgang ist geradeaus. Wenn ihr einen Hund habt, muss er angeleint sein.

☐ Du musst mit deinem Hund diesen Ausgang nehmen. Man soll auf dem Gras parken.

b) Deine Eltern können nicht so gut Englisch und haben noch einige Fragen.
Vervollständige das Gespräch.

VATER: Wo können wir denn hier parken? Ich kann nirgends einen Parkplatz sehen.
DU: _____
_____
_____

VATER: Soll ich dann geradeaus fahren?
DU: _____
_____
_____

MUTTER: Sollen wir den Hund besser im Auto lassen?
DU: Nein, wir können _____
_____

Step up!
- Antworten auf Deutsch geben zu müssen klingt eigentlich einfach. Achte aber darauf, das Schild nicht wörtlich zu übersetzen, sondern „richtiges" Deutsch zu verwenden.
- Vielleicht hilft es dir, deine Antworten laut vorzulesen (z. B. einem Freund) und zu prüfen, ob die deutschen Sätze auch natürlich klingen.
- Lies deine Antworten noch einmal aufmerksam durch: Hast du an alle gefragten Inhalte gedacht? Fällt dir noch ein Rechtschreibfehler auf? ■

36 a) Wenig später siehst du dieses Schild. Was sagst du zu deiner Mutter? Erkläre, wohin du gehen möchtest.

Mama, _____
_____
_____
_____
_____
_____
_____

*b) Deine Eltern, möchten gerne eine Kleinigkeit essen.
Du siehst das Schild dieses Cafés.
Vervollständige das Gespräch.

> **Step up!**
> - Hier gibt es evtl. englische Wörter, für die du keine direkte deutsche Entsprechung kennst. Erkläre in diesem Fall in eigenen Worten, was gemeint ist.
> - Denke daran, dass wir einige englische Wörter im Deutschen ebenfalls verwenden. ■

VATER: Ich habe jetzt keine Lust auf Eis. Wollen wir nicht lieber etwas „Richtiges" essen?

Du: Wir können _____

The Buttery.

VATER: Was ist *The Buttery*?

Du: _____

MUTTER: Kannst du uns sagen, was auf dem Schild steht?

Du: _____

VATER: Klingt gut, aber hoffentlich dauert das nicht zu lange. Wir wollen doch noch spazieren gehen. Was meinst du?

Du: _____

37 Es ist Mitte Juli als ihr (deine Eltern, dein Bruder und du) in Norfolk Urlaub macht. An einem Donnerstag um 11.30 steht ihr vor diesem Schild.
Ihr möchtet gerne nur das Schloss besuchen.
Gib deiner Familie alle wichtigen Informationen.

Step up!
- Meist enthält das Schild viel mehr Informationen als für die Aufgabe nötig sind. Markiere zuerst alle Teile des Schildes, die du für deine Antwort benötigst.
- Überlege, wie du diese Begriffe ins Deutsche übertragen kannst. Mache dir z. B. Stichpunkte neben dem Bild.
- Verwende diese Schlüsselwörter und schreibe auf, was du zu deinen Eltern sagen würdest. ∎

Topic 32: Can you help me? I don't speak German.

138 Du siehst amerikanische Jugendliche, die etwas hilflos auf dieses Schild schauen. Erkläre ihnen auf Englisch, was hier steht.
Einige schwierigere Wörter sind als Hilfe angegeben.

Step up!
- Überlege, wie du den Inhalt am besten mit den englischen Wörtern ausdrücken kannst, die du kennst.
- Dazu kann es hilfreich sein, unbekannte Ausdrücke zuerst im Deutschen zu umschreiben (z. B. täglich = jeden Tag). Versuche dann die deutsche Umschreibung ins Englische zu übertragen (jeden Tag = every day). ■

tower
Datum: z. B. 5th June
every day
go into / get into / enter / is open
Uhrzeit: z. B. 2 p.m.

Between _____ and _____
you can _____ the _____ until
_____ .

39 Du hast Besuch von deiner Freundin Eileen aus Irland. Gemeinsam seid ihr in Hamburg unterwegs und Eileen möchte gerne eine Hafenrundfahrt machen. Erkläre ihr auf Englisch, was die Fahrt für euch beide kostet und wann es losgehen kann.
(Hafen = *harbour*)

> **Step up!**
> - Markiere zuerst, welche Informationen auf dem Schild wichtig sind und übertrage sie ins Englische.
> - Oft kennst du vielleicht das passende englische Wort noch nicht, kannst aber mit anderen Wörtern erklären, was gemeint ist. Wenn du z. B. nicht weißt, was „Preis" heißt, kannst du auch sagen „*We must pay …*".
> - Versuche möglichst einfache englische Sätze zu formulieren; so kannst du Fehler vermeiden.
> - Denke daran, dass die Satzstellung im Englischen von der im Deutschen abweicht. Im Englischen gilt für einen Aussagesatz: *subject – verb – object*. ∎

We can _____
_____
_____
_____

*140 In der Nähe deines Wohnortes gibt es den Wildpark „Schloss am See".
In den Sommerferien triffst du eine Familie (zwei Erwachsene, ein kleines Kind) aus England, die diesen Prospekt bekommen hat. Sie fragen dich:
"Please can you tell us about 'Schloss am See'? What can you do there? How much does it cost and when is it open?"

a) Sieh dir den Prospekt zuerst ganz genau an. Streiche alle Informationen durch, die du in deiner Antwort nicht brauchst.

b) Was kannst du der Familie sagen?
Verwende die folgenden Wörter in deiner Antwort.

wildlife park – feed (= *füttern*) – birds of prey (= *Greifvögel*) – show – playground

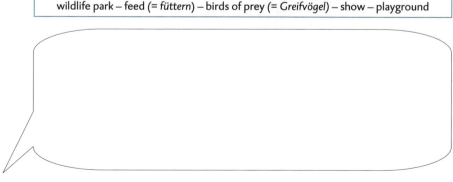

Topic 33: The country teenager

41 Lies den Blog von Amy, die von ihrem Alltag erzählt.
Beantworte dann die Fragen auf Deutsch.

> **Step up!**
> - Lies dir den Text einmal komplett durch, damit du weißt, worum es ungefähr geht.
> - Lies dann jeweils eine Frage und suche die Textstellen, in denen du die Antwort findest. Markiere diese Stellen farbig und verwende für jede Frage eine neue Farbe.
> - Achte darauf, wirklich nur die Inhalte zu übertragen, nach denen gefragt wird. ■

Amy's Blog.co.uk

Blog archive
November
December
January
▶ Tuesday 4th

My Life in the Country
Tuesday, 4th January

I live in a nice house in a small village but my house is not in the middle of it. There isn't a school bus that goes to my village but there is a small station. Every morning I put on my school uniform and walk 20 minutes to the station. In bad weather my father drives me there. At the station I meet other pupils from my school and we all wait for the small train to Whitby. When I get to Whitby, I have to walk for fifteen minutes up a hill to the school.

I have fun at school because I see my friends. At the end of the day I have to go home again on the train.

I use the internet a lot to chat to friends and I text people, too. I sometimes go to pop concerts with my friends but that means we have to go to Newcastle, about 90 minutes away, or Manchester, about three hours away. When I want to go shopping with my friends, I take the small train to the next big town, about 45 minutes away.

I like living in the country but my parents have to drive me to a lot of things.

Posted by Amy at 10:44 AM   4 comments

Vocabulary
station: *Bahnhof*; (to) text: *eine Nachricht/SMS schreiben/senden*

116 / Mediation

a) Wovon handelt der Text?

_____
_____
_____

b) Erkläre, wie Amy in die Schule kommt.
   Die Zeichnungen zeigen dir, was deine Antwort unbedingt enthalten sollte:

   [STATION — 20 minutes — 15 minutes]

c) Wie kann Amy Kontakt mit Freunden halten?

_____
_____
_____

d) Wie schwierig ist es, zu Popkonzerten zu gehen und warum?

_____
_____
_____
_____

Topic 34: My London walk

42 Toni aus Deutschland ist in London. Sie schickt ihrem Freund Sammy in den USA diese E-Mail. Kannst du Sammy helfen, Tonis E-Mail zu verstehen?
Vervollständige den Text auf Englisch. Manchmal musst du mehrere Wörter pro Lücke eintragen.

Toni is _____ about _____ _____ London. She wants to tell her _____ about _____ because _____ is going to _____, too.

143 Du bist Toni. In der Jugendherberge, in der du übernachtest, triffst du am Abend Jugendliche aus Japan, die gerade angekommen sind. Sie fragen dich nach Tipps. Sage ihnen, wo für dich die Mitte von London ist, wo man einkaufen kann, und wo man viele reiche Leute in London treffen könnte.

*144 Am nächsten Tag möchte Toni eine Stadtrundfahrt machen.
Während sie wartet, hört sie eine Werbung.
Eine Touristin steht alleine in der Schlange und wendet sich an Toni.
Track 48 Übernimm Tonis Rolle und beantworte die Frage auf Deutsch.

TOURISTIN: Entschuldigung, du bist auch aus Deutschland, oder? Ich habe gerade gehört wie du Deutsch gesprochen hast.
Kannst du mir bitte erklären, was der Mann gerade gesagt hat? Mein Englisch ist nicht so gut.

DU: Ja, wir kommen aus Berlin. Ich werde versuchen, zu erklären, was der Mann gesagt hat.

145 Du bist Sammy und antwortest auf Tonis E-Mail. Bedanke dich und schreibe, welche zwei Dinge aus Tonis E-Mail du unbedingt sehen möchtest, wenn du nach London kommst. Sage auch, warum sie dich interessieren.
(*I would like to* ... = ich möchte gerne ...; *because* = weil)

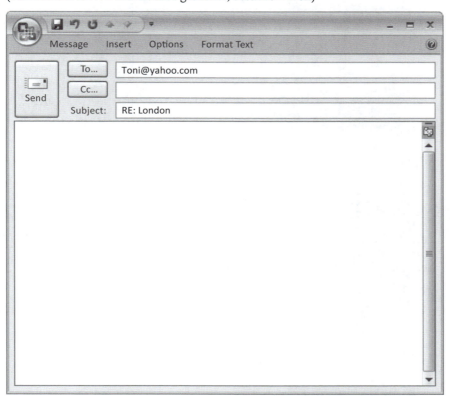

146 Toni hat bei ihrem Spaziergang einige Fotos gemacht.
  a) Kannst du sie in die richtige Reihenfolge bringen? Fülle die Tabelle aus.

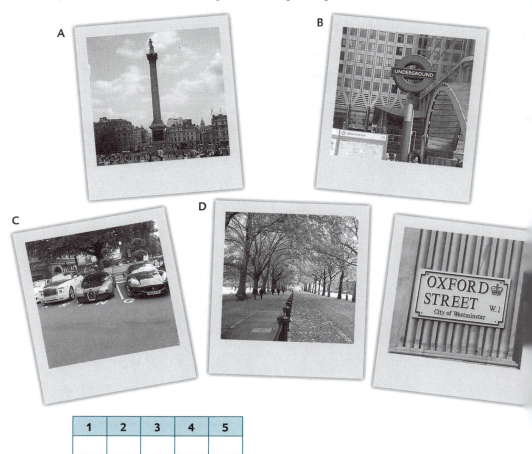

1	2	3	4	5

b) Toni möchte Sammy die Fotos schicken, hat aber vergessen, etwas dazu zu schreiben. Schreibe zu jedem Foto einen passenden Satz auf Englisch.
Drei Sätze sind teilweise vorgegeben.

A	
B	
C	this big hotel.
D	This is
E	

Topic 35: Sorry, I don't understand!

147 Sophia und Robin müssen mit ihrem Lehrer nach der Schule noch etwas besprechen, aber sie haben ihre englischen Austauschpartner dabei. Sophia schlägt vor, Kim und Dave später im Café gegenüber der Schule zu treffen.
Lies den Dialog. Du bist Sophia, die Dolmetscherin. Hake ab (✓), was du sagst.

KIM: Where's Sophia, Dave? Oh, there she is. Sophia! Sophia! Come here – quick! I don't understand what the woman is saying.

KELLNERIN: *Was möchtet ihr?*

SOPHIA: She wants to know …
- [ ] what time it is.
- [ ] what you would like.
- [ ] do you like him?

KIM: A glass of water, please.

DAVE: And a large cola for me.

SOPHIA:
- [ ] *Sie möchte ein Glas Wasser und er möchte eine große Cola.*
- [ ] *Er möchte ein Wasser und sie möchte eine Cola.*
- [ ] *Sie möchte eine Flasche Wasser und eine Cola.*

KELLNERIN: *Möchte sie ein großes Glas Wasser oder ein kleines?*

SOPHIA:
- [ ] How do you want the water?
- [ ] Do you want a large or a small glass of water?
- [ ] Is his water big or small?

KIM: A large glass of water, please.

DAVE: And, can I have some ice in my drink?

SOPHIA:
- [ ] *Ein großes Glas Wasser mit Eiswürfeln.*
- [ ] *Die Getränke mit Eiswürfeln.*
- [ ] *Ein großes Glas Wasser und Eiswürfel in der Cola.*

148 Später will Dave ein Geschenk für seine Mutter kaufen. Robin und Dave gehen in einen Laden, der Schokolade verkauft.
Du bist Robin und musst zwischen Dave und dem Verkäufer dolmetschen.

ROBIN: *Mein Freund will ein Geschenk für seine Mutter kaufen.*

VERKÄUFER: *Was möchte er denn für sie kaufen?*

ROBIN: _____

DAVE: I'd like some chocolates. But I don't have a lot of money.

ROBIN: _____

VERKÄUFER: *Bei diesen hier kosten 100 Gramm nur 6,35 €.*

ROBIN: _____

DAVE: € 6.35!! I only have € 4. Can I buy anything for € 4?

ROBIN: _____

VERKÄUFER: *Leider nicht. Aber der Supermarkt dort hat auch Schokolade.*

ROBIN: _____

DAVE: Can we go there, now?

***149** Während die Jungen Schokolade suchen, kaufen die Mädchen ein T-Shirt für Kim. Du bist Sophia. Was sagst du?

VERKÄUFERIN: *Kann ich euch helfen?*

SOPHIA: *Diese T-Shirts gefallen meiner Freundin.*

VERKÄUFERIN: *Welche Größe hat sie?*

SOPHIA: _____

KIM: I usually need a small size.

SOPHIA: _____.

VERKÄUFERIN: *Das ist ihre Größe. Sie kann es dort anprobieren.*

SOPHIA: _____

KIM: It's the right size. Is there a blue one?

SOPHIA: _____

VERKÄUFERIN: *Nein, leider nicht. Wir haben diese T-Shirts nur in Weiß oder Grün. Soll ich sie euch zeigen?*

SOPHIA: _____

KIM: Only the white T-shirt – I don't like green – and can you ask her how much the T-shirts are?

SOPHIA: _____

VERKÄUFERIN: *Sie kosten 25 €.*

SOPHIA: _____

Topic 36: Student exchange

Du nimmst an einem Schüleraustausch mit eurer englischen Partnerschule teil. Während des Aufenthaltes macht ihr viele Ausflüge und lernt interessante Menschen kennen. Manche deutschen Schüler können aber noch nicht so gut Englisch. Kannst du weiterhelfen?

50 Heute Morgen seid ihr in Cornwall und am Nachmittag fahrt ihr weiter nach London. Morgens hört ihr im Radio den Wetterbericht für den Tag.
Deine deutsche Freundin hat aber nicht alles verstanden. Erkläre ihr, mit welchem Wetter ihr rechnen könnt.

Step up!
- Hier musst du eine **Hörverstehensaufgabe** lösen und die Antwort ins Deutsche übertragen.
- Sieh dir zuerst die Aufgabe genau an, damit du weißt, auf was du beim Hören besonders achten musst. Hier ist das z. B. das Wetter in Cornwall und London.
- Mache dir während des Hörens Notizen zum Wetter an diesen Orten auf Englisch. Überlege erst nach dem Hören, wie du die Antwort auf Deutsch formulieren würdest. ■

_____
_____
_____
_____

51 In deiner Gastfamilie lernst du die Amerikanerin Mary kennen, die Tante deines Austauschpartners, die gerade zu Besuch ist. Sie erzählt dir von ihrem ungewöhnlichen Beruf. Am nächsten Tag sprichst du mit deinen Freunden über Mary. Erkläre auf Deutsch:
- was sie genau tut,
- warum sie ihren Beruf mag,
- und was sie daran nicht mag.

_____
_____
_____
_____

152 Heute ist euer letzter Tag in England. Im Bus macht die englische Lehrerin gerade eine Durchsage. Du hast sie gut verstanden, aber dein deutscher Freund hatte Probleme.

Track 51

a) Damit du nichts vergisst, schreibst du dir das Wichtigste sofort in dein Notizbuch (auf Englisch).

Why is the bus stopping?	Extra information
Where is the bus?	
Meet – where? when?	Problems?

b) Erkläre deinem Freund auf Deutsch, was für ihn wichtig ist.

Topic 36: Student exchange 125

53 Einige Monate später kommt dein Austauschpartner Jack nach Deutschland. Nach seinem Besuch fahrt ihr gemeinsam zu seiner Familie nach England. Auf dem Weg dorthin hört ihr drei Durchsagen und Jack braucht deine Hilfe.

a) Höre dir die erste Durchsage an und erkläre Jack, um was es geht.
Fülle die Lücken mit passenden englischen Wörtern.
Our _____ is _____ late.

b) Jack fragt dich: "Can I get something to eat and drink on the train?"
Wie antwortest du ihm?
_____, _____. You can _____ hot and cold
_____
near the front of _____

c) Sieh dir eure Bordkarten an. Erkläre Jack, was ihr machen müsst.
Hier sind einige englische Wörter, die du in deiner Antwort verwenden solltest: *gate* (Gate), *row* (Reihe), *wait* (warten)

We have to go to _____. Because we sit
_____ we must _____ until the other
_____ in _____
get onto the _____.

Topic 37: School project

154 a) Du nimmst an einem Projekt mit einer Partnerschule in Amerika teil. Dafür sollt ihr eure Schule und alle, die dort arbeiten, vorstellen.
Ihr wollt Steckbriefe von einigen Lehrern erstellen.
Dein Freund führt ein Gespräch mit eurer Englischlehrerin Frau Schmidt.
Du musst danach das Formular, das die Amerikaner geschickt haben, auf Englisch ausfüllen. Du kannst Kurzantworten schreiben.

Track 55

Teacher Profile

Name: _____

Age: _____

From: _____

Married ☐
Single ☐

Children: _____

Teaches: _____

Free time activities: _____
_____

Pets: _____

Other languages: _____

Husband's / wife's
name and job: _____

Three things to take
to a desert island: _____

b) Höre dir das Interview noch einmal an und lies die Informationen, die du gerade in das „Teacher Profile" geschrieben hast, noch einmal durch.
Verwende diese Informationen und schreibe einen kurzen Text über Frau Schmidt auf Englisch. Schreibe ganze Sätze.

_____
_____
_____
_____
_____
_____
_____

c) Frau Schmidt betreut das Amerika-Projekt und hat ein Arbeitsblatt verteilt. Stelle dir vor, dass du das Telefongespräch auf der CD führst. Höre es sorgfältig an und mache dir Notizen zu den wichtigsten Punkten, die du deiner Klasse sagen wirst.

School Project: Task 2	Notes about Chelsea
Phone your American partner. Find out about where he/she lives. Tell your class tomorrow about your partner **in German**. Good luck!	

d) In der nächsten Ausgabe der Schülerzeitung sollen einige amerikanische Schüler vorgestellt werden.
Verwende deine Notizen und schreibe einen kurzen Text über Chelsea.

_____
_____
_____
_____
_____
_____

Writing –
Strategien zum Kompetenzbereich Textproduktion

Es gibt viele verschiedene Arten, wie man üben kann, etwas auf Englisch zu **schreiben**. Zuerst musst du nur Lücken ausfüllen oder Sätze vervollständigen. Dann steigerst du dich langsam und du schreibst zuerst einzelne Sätze, dann kleine Texte selbst. Die Aufgaben am Anfang jedes *Topics* sind leichter, danach werden sie langsam anspruchsvoller. Kniffligere Aufgaben sind mit einem Sternchen (*) gekennzeichnet. Beim Schreiben ist es wichtig, sich **genügend Zeit** zu nehmen und **schrittweise** vorzugehen:

- ■ Sieh dir zuerst die Aufgabe genau an. Oft gehören Bilder oder kurze Texte zur **Aufgabenstellung**, die du zunächst verstehen musst.

- ■ Mache dann eine **Ideensammlung** auf einem Notizzettel und schreibe damit die erste Version deines Textes.

- ■ Vergleiche diese noch einmal mit dem Arbeitsauftrag. Passt der Inhalt auch genau zur Aufgabe? Vielleicht musst du die erste Fassung deines Textes **überarbeiten**.

- ■ Lies dir deinen Text mehrmals durch und versuche selbst, Fehler zu finden.

Topic 38: Land's End

Note
Die beiden Fotos sind von Land's End. Das ist in Südengland. Es ist der westlichste Ort in Großbritannien. John o'Groats – der nördlichste Ort – ist in Schottland.

155 Sieh dir die beiden Fotos des Wegweisers *(signpost)* genau an.
Vervollständige die Sätze.

> **Step up!**
> Manchmal kommen in den Texten, die du schreiben möchtest, **Zahlen** vor:
> - Schreibe Zahlen bis zwölf in einem Wort (z. B. *twelve*).
> - Schreibe größere Zahlen als Ziffer (z. B. 150). ■

a) The date in the photo is _____.

b) It is _____ miles to New York.

c) There are _____ people near the signpost.

d) The _____ in the white T-shirt is _____ letters on the signpost.

e) The other people are _____ her.

f) I think it is a _____ day. *(Wetter)*

g) I can _____ the sea behind *(hinter)* the _____.

56 Beantworte die folgenden Fragen.
Schreibe deine Meinung und vervollständige die Sätze.

a) Why is this place called Land's End?
   I think this place is called Land's End because _____
   _____

b) What two things can you put on the signpost?
   I can put _____
   _____ on the signpost.

57 a) Sieh dir das Bild genau an. Notiere, was auf dem Bild zu sehen ist (wenn möglich auf Englisch).

> **Step up!**
> Aufgaben im Bereich *Writing* beziehen sich oft auf **Bilder**. Sieh dir das Foto zuerst gut an. Folgende Fragen können dir helfen, auf alles Wichtige zu achten. (Es ist nicht schlimm, wenn du noch nicht alles auf Englisch ausdrücken kannst.)
> - Was ist im Vordergrund/im Hintergrund zu sehen?
> - Wo könnte das Bild aufgenommen sein? Wer ist zu sehen?
> - Kannst du etwas über das Wetter, die Jahreszeit sagen? ∎

Hintergrund (background):

T-Shirt text:

Vordergrund (foreground):

Wetter (weather), Jahreszeit (season):

Ort (place):

b) Du bist einer der drei Radfahrer auf dem Foto. Die Familie im Hintergrund kommt näher und möchte gerne wissen, was ihr macht.
Der Junge stellt dir einige Fragen. Was sagst du zu ihm?
Schreibe deine Antwort in ganzen Sätzen.

BOY: Where are you cycling to?
YOU: _____
_____

BOY: Where is John o'Groats?
YOU: _____

(*Schottland* = Scotland)

BOY: How many miles is it to John o'Groats?
YOU: _____

BOY: Where are your bags?
YOU: _____

(*z. B. Auto eines Freundes*)

> **Step up!**
> Lies dir stets die Aufgabenstellung genau durch. Hier musst du dich in eine Person auf dem Foto hineinversetzen.
> - Sieh dir die Radfahrer und die Familie auf dem Foto nochmals an. Der Text auf dem T-Shirt hilft dir, die Lücken zu füllen.
> - Lies dir den ganzen Lückentext durch, bevor du mit dem Ausfüllen beginnst. Aus den Antworten des Jungen kannst du oft ableiten, was in deinen Lücken stehen muss. ∎

c) Du willst einem Freund bzw. einer Freundin in den USA das Foto der Radfahrer per E-Mail senden und erzählen, was du erlebt hast. Bevor du mit der E-Mail beginnst, lies dir die Hinweise in „*Step up!*" zum Verfassen von E-Mails im Englischen genau durch und sieh dir das Beispiel an.

> **Step up!**
> Egal ob du einen **Brief** oder eine **E-Mail** schreibst, zuerst musst du überlegen, ob du an einen guten Freund schreibst oder ob es sich um einen offiziellen Brief handelt.
> - Briefe an Freunde und Verwandte beginnst du z. B. mit „*Hi Sam,*" oder „*Dear Aunt Jane,*". Am Ende kannst du z. B. „*Best wishes,*" oder „*Love,*" schreiben („*Love*" verwendet man aber nicht in Briefen zwischen Jungen / Männern). Vergiss nicht, danach ein Komma zu setzen.
> - Anders als im Deutschen beginnt man englische Briefe und E-Mails mit einem Großbuchstaben.
> - In E-Mail-Formularen trägst du bei „*To*" die Adresse der Person ein, an die die E-Mail geht. Unter „*Subject*" schreibst du in wenigen Worten, worum es in der Mail geht. ∎

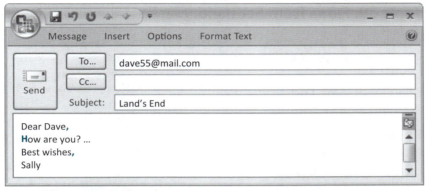

Beispiel für eine E-Mail

Hier findest du Ideen für den Inhalt deiner E-Mail.
Schreibe einen Satz zu jeder Frage in der Tabelle.

The photo:	Where are you? Is it a nice place? Are there many houses here?
The weather:	Today – Is it warm? Is it sunny? (1 sentence)
The people on bikes:	How many people are on bikes? What are the people wearing? Where are they going to? How far is it?
The other people:	Are there a lot of people here? Who are the people?
Words to help: helmet *(Helm)* – away *(weit weg)* – tourist *(Tourist)*	

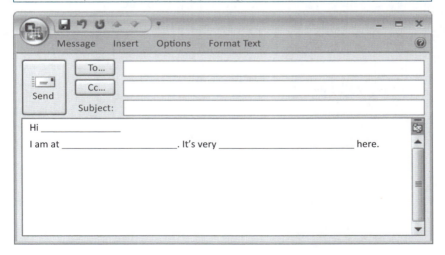

Topic 39: Fiona from Scotland

158 Verwende die vorgegebenen Wörter und schreibe eine kurze Geschichte auf Englisch.
Fülle die Lücken mit den richtigen Wörtern.

> **Step up!**
> In diesem *Topic* musst du – wie bei einer Mediation – vorgegebene deutsche Wörter ins Englische übertragen.
> - Meist benötigst du zusätzlich noch weitere Wörter, um ganze Sätze zu bilden.
> - Überlege zuerst, welche Wörter jeweils noch fehlen: ein Verb, eine Präposition oder ein Substantiv? Denke auch an die englische Wortstellung (subject – verb – object). ■

Beispiel:
Fiona / Schottland / Schottland / See
__Fiona__ lives in __Scotland__. In __Scotland__ there are lots of __lakes__.

a) *Fiona / Bruder / Schwester*
   _____ has got a _____ and a _____.

b) *Name / Andrew / Schwester / sein*
   Her brother's _____ is _____.
   Her _____ name _____ Lilly.

c) *wohnen / Haus / Scotland*
   They _____ in a _____ in _____.

159 Schreibe mithilfe der Wörter in Klammern eine kurze Geschichte über Fiona, Andrew und die Schule. Diesmal musst du keinen Lückentext ausfüllen, sondern selbst ganze Sätze schreiben.

a) *(Schule / Edinburgh)*
   _____

b) *(Fiona: Lieblingsfach Englisch / Andrew: ...)*
   _____

c) *(erste bzw. letzte Unterrichtsstunde / Beginn, Ende)*
   _____

60 Hier ist eine Geschichte über eine Geburtstagsüberraschung.
Fülle die Lücken mit Wörtern aus der Zeichnung.

Step up!
- In einem **Lückentext** darf meist jedes Wort nur einmal verwendet werden. Falls du denkst, dass zwei Wörter gleich gut in eine Lücke passen, trage sie zuerst nur mit Bleistift ein und lese weiter. Nach und nach wird klar, welche Möglichkeit richtig ist.
- Überlege bei den Verben, welche Form du verwenden musst. Suche Hinweise aus dem Text: Steht z. B. vor der Lücke *he/she/it*, so musst du ein „s" an das Verb anhängen *(he walks)*. Steht eine Form von *to be* vor der Lücke, so musst du die *ing*-Form *(progressive*-Form) verwenden: z. B. *I am ...* → *I am writing*
- Überlege bei Substantiven, ob du den Plural oder den Singular brauchst, z. B. *He has got two ...* → *He has got two presents*). ■

Fiona goes to her _____ and _____ outside.
She _____ a woman. The woman is _____ away
from her _____. Fiona goes to the front _____,
she _____ it and there she _____ a big box
_____ her name on it. On the box there are the _____
'Happy Birthday, Fiona'. Fiona _____ surprises and this really
_____ a surprise.

161 Nessie ist sehr freundlich gewesen und hat dir viele deutsche Wörter verraten, sodass du eine Geschichte über sie schreiben kannst. Aber pass auf, sie hat dir zwei Wörter zu viel aufgeschrieben. Vervollständige ihre Geschichte.

Loch Ness is in Scotland. It _____ famous for its monster. The monster's name is Nessie. _____ about a monster in Loch Ness are not _____. _____ story is _____ 1400 years old. This story is about a famous saint (= *Heiliger*) that _____ a monster at Loch Ness.
The name "Nessie" isn't _____. It is from a newspaper in 1933.
There are photos of Nessie but they are _____ good photos.
People _____ that Nessie has got a _____ neck and a hump (= *Buckel*).
What do you think? Is there a monster in Loch Ness?

Topic 40: I live here

62 Wer lebt wo in *Field Lane*? Sieh das Bild genau an und dann die Lösung. Schreibe einen Hinweis für jedes Haus und seinen Eigentümer, sodass jemand das Rätsel „Wer lebt wo?" lösen könnte, wenn er deine Sätze verwendet.

House	Fiona	Zoe	Joe	Peter	Katie	Dr. Charles	Mrs Bruce
1	✓	✗	✗	✗	✗	✗	✗
2	✗	✗	✓	✗	✗	✗	✗
3	✗	✗	✗	✗	✗	✗	✓
4	✗	✓	✗	✗	✗	✗	✗
5	✗	✗	✗	✗	✗	✓	✗
6	✗	✗	✗	✓	✗	✗	✗
7	✗	✗	✗	✗	✓	✗	✗

a) Fiona's children __have got bikes._____ .

b) Zoe has got a _____, a _____ and _____ in her garden.

c) Joe has got a _____ in his _____.

d) Peter lives between *(zwischen)* the house with _____ and the house with _____.

e) Katie's house is opposite *(gegenüber)* _____.

f) Dr Charles lives _____.

g) _____.

163 Denke darüber nach, wo du lebst. Schreibe über dein Haus, als ob du ein Rätsel für jemanden machen würdest, der es finden muss.

a) My house has got _____ windows. *(Fenster)*

b) _____. *(Garten)*

c) _____. *(Farbe)*

d) _____.

***164** Sieh das Foto genau an. Beschreibe das mittlere Haus mit so vielen Einzelheiten wie möglich.

_____

_____

_____

_____

_____

_____

Topic 41: An e-mail to …

65 Beantworte die Fragen in ganzen Sätzen und achte auf die richtige Schreibung.

> **Step up!**
>
> Kennst du die Regeln für die **Groß- und Kleinschreibung**? Wenn du nicht mehr weißt, wann man etwas im Englischen großschreibt, kannst du hier noch einmal nachlesen.
>
> - Wörter am Anfang von Sätzen: <u>Their</u> house is nice.
> - Eigennamen und I: Can <u>Eva</u> and <u>I</u> watch TV?
> - Ortsnamen und Straßennamen: We live in <u>Dover</u>. Anna lives in <u>West Street</u>.
> - Ländernamen und Adjektive, die Länder bezeichnen: James comes from <u>America</u>. He's <u>American</u>.
> - Wochentage und Monatsnamen: They play tennis on <u>Tuesdays</u>. My birthday is in <u>October</u>.
> - Titel von Büchern, Filmen usw. (aber „and", „the" usw. werden, wenn sie nicht am Anfang stehen, kleingeschrieben): Sue is watching <u>The Titanic</u>. Martin is reading <u>Travel the World</u>.
> - Einige Abkürzungen: Have <u>Mr</u> and <u>Mrs</u> Lucas got a car? / OK
> - Im Brief das erste Wort nach der Anrede (nach dem Komma): Dear Thomas, <u>Can</u> you come to my party? …
> - Mum, Dad, Aunt/Uncle (+ Namen), wenn sie statt des Namens einer Person verwendet werden: Have you got <u>Mum</u>'s camera? No, <u>Uncle</u> James has it. ■

a) Where do you live? *(street and town)*
   I live in _____

b) What is your favourite day? My favourite day is _____

c) When is you birthday? *(month)*
   My birthday is in _____

d) What is the name of your favourite pop group?
   _____

e) Tom Woods and his family now live in London. How do you start a letter to his parents?
   _____

f) What is the name of your favourite book or film? _____

166 Sieh die die Bilder genau an. Beantworte die Fragen in ganzen Sätzen.

a) Where is the bookshop?

b) Whose birthday is it? Who is the present from?

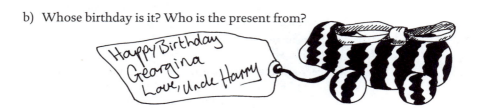

c) Where does Mike come from?

167 a) Schreibe Sallys E-Mail an Peter richtig. Verwende Großbuchstaben, wo sie erforderlich sind. Denke an die richtige Zeichensetzung.

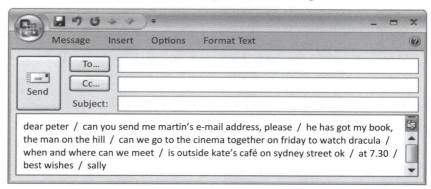

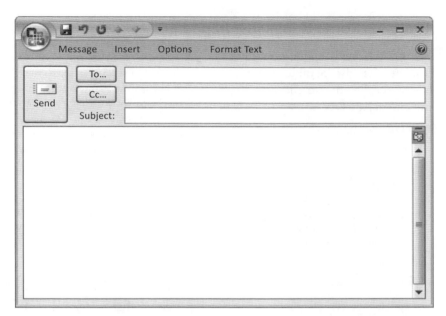

b) Du bist Peter. Antworte auf Sallys E-Mail. Natürlich musst du Informationen hinzufügen. Versuche eine gute E-Mail zu schreiben und denke daran, wann Großbuchstaben verwendet werden.

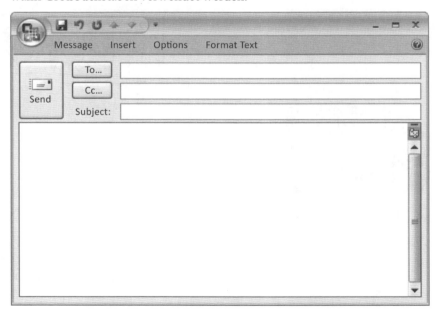

Topic 42: Some things just happen

168 Kannst du Geschichten interessanter machen? Sieh dir die Bilder an und beschreibe die unterstrichenen Wörter mit einem Adjektiv.

Step up!
Wenn du einen Satz interessanter machen möchtest, musst du überlegen, welche zusätzlichen Informationen du geben könntest.
- Suche nach Adjektiven (sie bestimmen Nomen näher): *book* → *new book, old book, interesting book.*
- Ergänze zu Personennamen ein Nomen, das eine zusätzliche Information gibt: *John* → *my friend John.* Füge wieder Adjektive hinzu: *my old / best friend John* ■

a) There is a <u>window</u>, over there.
_____

b) He sees a <u>bridge</u>.
_____

c) She works in a <u>shop</u>.
_____

d) Carol has got a <u>car</u>.

_____

e) There is a <u>dog</u> in the <u>garden</u>.
_____

Topic 42: Some things just happen 143

69 Schaue dir die Bilder an und schreibe die Geschichte dazu.
Verwende die Wörter in Klammern.

(warm / sonnig)

It is a _____

_____

(Lilly ruft wen an? / Tennis spielen?)

She asks _____ : " _____

_____ ?"

(Tennis / Garten)

Lilly and _____

_____

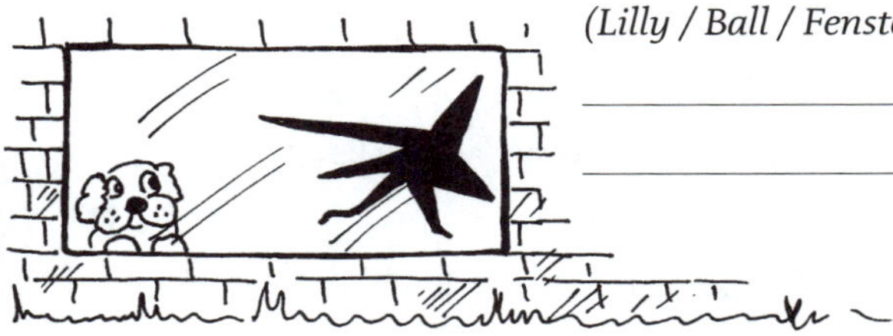

(Lilly / Ball / Fenster)

_____

_____

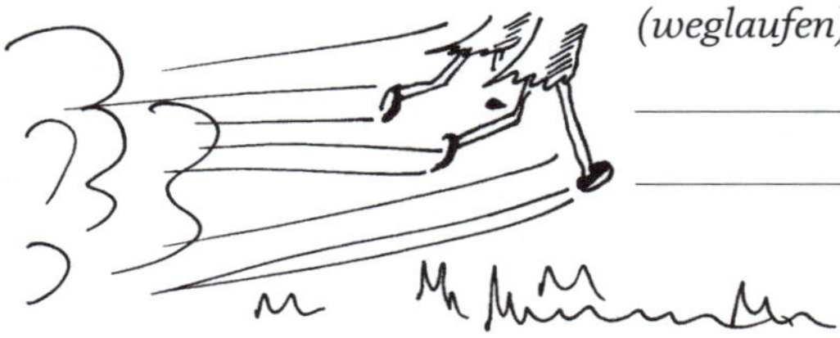

(weglaufen)

_____

_____

*170 a) Sieh dir die Bilder an und vervollständige die Geschichte in eigenen Worten. Vorsicht, die Bilder sind durcheinander geraten.
(Schwert = *sword*)

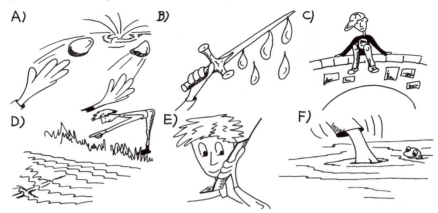

Cal's village is small and sometimes there's nothing to do there. Today, Cal's parents are working and his sister is playing outside.

Cal _____ his friend, Tony, and asks him to meet him at the bridge. At two o'clock, Tony is _____

_____.

"What can we do?" Cal asks Tony.

"Let's go to the river," Tony answers.

After ten minutes the boys stop walking and _____

_____.

Suddenly, Cal sees something _____.

"What's that, Tony? Over there. Can you see it?" Cal asks.

"There's nothing there, Cal," says Tony.

"I'm going to see what it is," Cal says. He _____

into the river and finds _____.

b) In welche Reihenfolge gehören die Bilder in der Geschichte?

1	2	3	4	5	6

Topic 43: Happy birthday, Luke!

71 Schreibe fünf Sätze über Luke Scotts Geburtstag mithilfe der Wörter in Klammern.
Füge Informationen hinzu, um interessante und vollständige Sätze zu bilden.

a) *(Luke / birthday)*
Today, _____

b) *(12 years old / presents)*
_____

c) *(sister's present / CD)*
_____

d) *(go / cinema / friends)*
_____

e) *(has / day)*
_____

72 Sieh die Bilder und die Wörter in Klammern an.
Vervollständige die Geschichte über Lukes Geburtstag.
Überlege dir zusätzliche Informationen. Antworte im *present tense*.

(birthday / skateboard)
It is _____ today.
He has got _____
for _____ birthday.

(happy)
_____ with his
_____ .

(park / have lots of fun)
He is _____ .
He is _____ .

146 | Writing

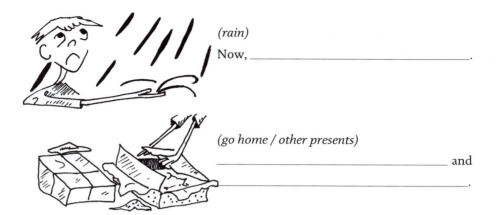

(rain)
Now, _____.

(go home / other presents)
_____ and
_____.

173 Lukes Tante Annie aus Edinburgh hat sich in einer Radiosendung am frühen Abend ein Lied für Luke gewünscht und ihm so zum Geburtstag gratuliert. Sie konnte am 16. März nicht in Liverpool sein, weil sie arbeiten musste.
Für den Musikwunsch hat sie ein Formular im Internet ausgefüllt. Was hat sie geschrieben? Die Informationen, die du brauchst, stehen im ganzen Kapitel. Manchmal musst du noch etwas ergänzen. Fülle das Formular für Annie aus.

Music wish from:
Name: _____ From: _____
To:
Name: _____
Address: _____
Why: _____
_____
Song / music type request: _____
Message: _____
_____
Time for song: _____ Date: _____

Topic 44: Free time

74 a) In einem Internetforum wollen sechs Leute schreiben, was sie gerne in ihrer Freizeit machen. Auf der Startseite stehen bis jetzt aber nur ganz wenige Informationen zu jeder Person. Welche Bilder und welche Wörter könnten die Jugendlichen in ihren Texten verwenden?
Verbinde die Wörter in der Liste mit den dazugehörenden Bildern und einer Person.

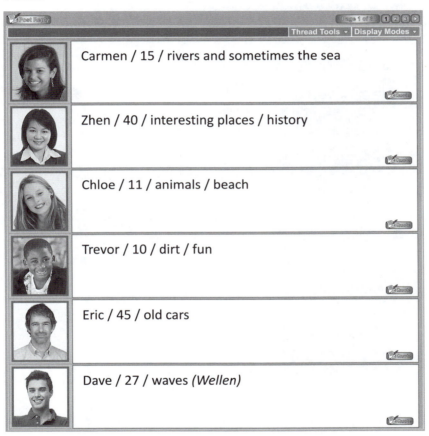

Words the people can use in their texts:

surfing	canoeing	mountain biking
sightseeing	driving	horse riding

148 Writing

Name	Carmen	Zhen	Chloe	Trevor	Eric	Dave
Photo						
Word		sight-seeing				

b) Kannst du über diese Personen einen kurzen Text schreiben?
Verwende die Informationen der letzen beiden Seiten.

Carmen: Carmen is _____ years old. She likes _____ _____. She enjoys _____ _____.

> **Step up!**
> So kannst du sprachliche Fehler in deinen Texten vermeiden:
> - Schreibe kurze einfache Sätze. Achte auf die Satzstellung im Englischen.
> - Verwende nur Wörter, bei denen du sicher bist, dass die Bedeutung passt und dass du ihre Schreibung kennst. ■

Chloe: _____

Eric: _____

c) Zhen und Trevor wollen im Onlineforum von sich erzählen.
Schreibe, was sie sagen und füge wo möglich zusätzliche Einzelheiten hinzu.

Zhen: My name is _____

Trevor: _____

175 Versuche mit weiteren Informationen deine Sätze interessanter zu machen. Sieh das Foto an und kreise bei jedem Satz das *kursiv* geschriebene Wort ein, das du verwenden könntest, um den Satz interessanter zu machen.

a) It is a picture of a shop. → It is a picture of *a shoe / an insect* shop.

b) There is a scorpion on the wall. → There is a *big / small* scorpion on the wall.

c) There are shoes on the wall. → There are *two / three* shoes on the wall.

d) Scorpion is a shop in London. → Scorpion is a *big / small* shop in London.

e) Schreibe deinen eigenen Satz über die Schilder an der Wand über dem Geschäft. Du musst die Schilder nicht übersetzen.

_____
_____
_____

f) Gehst du in deiner Freizeit gerne einkaufen?
Schreibe drei Sätze mithilfe der vorgegebenen Fragen.

Do you like shopping?

Yes!	No!
Where and what for? Who with?	Why not? What do you like?

_____

_____

76 a) Du möchtest ebenfalls in einem Online-Netzwerk etwas über dich schreiben.
Was kannst du über deine Freizeit sagen? Lege zuerst eine Mindmap an und schreibe auf, was du gerne tust.
Sieh dir das Beispiel an:

> **Step up!**
> Bevor man einen Text schreiben kann, braucht man gute **Ideen**:
> • Beginne nicht sofort mit dem Schreiben. Sammle zuerst Ideen, z. B. in einer Mindmap.
> • Gehe von deinem Thema aus (z. B. Kino) und überlege, <u>wo</u> dies zu finden ist, <u>wann</u>, <u>wie oft</u> und <u>mit wem</u> du dort bist und <u>was</u> dir daran gefällt.
> • Vielleicht merkst du bei der Ideensammlung, dass dir nicht genug zu einem Thema einfällt. Versuche es dann mit einem anderen Thema und mache eine neue Stoffsammlung. ■

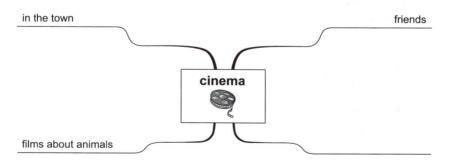

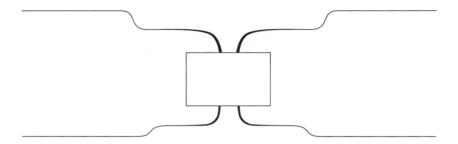

b) Verwende nun die Informationen aus deiner Mindmap und schreibe einen Text über deine Freizeit. Sieh dir zuerst das Beispiel an.

Step up!

Wenn dein Text fertig ist, lies ihn dir mehrmals durch und versuche ihn selbst zu verbessern.

- Achte beim ersten Lesen auf den **Inhalt**: Hast du die Aufgabe richtig beantwortet? Vergleiche mit der Aufgabenstellung.
- Sieh dir beim zweiten Lesen die **Schreibung** der Wörter an. Entdeckst du einen Fehler?
- Dann ist die **Grammatik** an der Reihe: Hast du an der richtigen Stelle *simple present (I go)* und *present progressive (I'm going)* verwendet? Ist bei der *simple*-Form bei jedem Verb in der 3. Person ein „s" *(he goes, she says)* ? Hast du die richtigen Pluralformen verwendet *(child – children)*? Stimmt die Wortstellung?
- Meist ist es einfacher, die Fehler in einem fremden Text zu sehen als im eigenen. Wenn möglich, tausche deinen Text mit einem Freund aus und korrigiert euch gegenseitig. ■

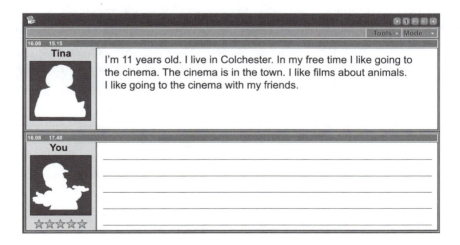

77 Sieh dir die Anzeige des Freizeitparks Seaview Fun Park an und lies die Fragen.
Schreibe einen Dialog zwischen dir und einem Freund.
Schreibe vier Fragen und vier Antworten.

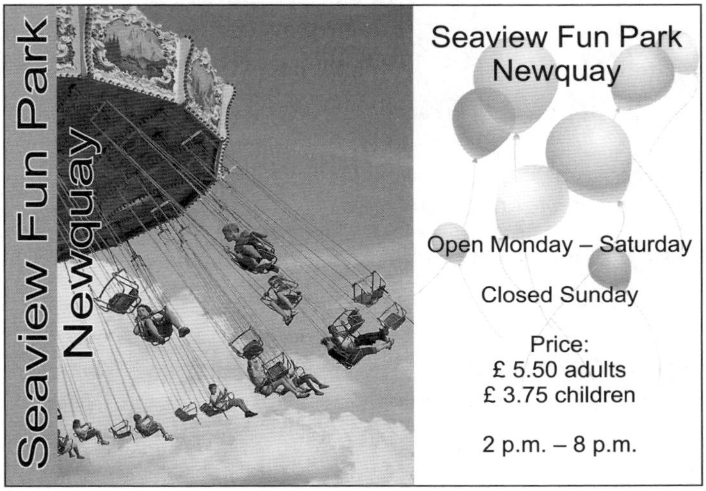

**Seaview Fun Park
Newquay**

Open Monday – Saturday

Closed Sunday

Price:
£ 5.50 adults
£ 3.75 children

2 p.m. – 8 p.m.

→ Wo?
→ Wann?
→ Preise?
→ Öffnungs-
  zeiten?

YOU: _____ is the Seaview Fun Park?
FRIEND: It _____
YOU: _____?
FRIEND: _____
_____
YOU: _____?
FRIEND: _____
_____
YOU: _____?
FRIEND: _____
_____

Topic 45: The Eden Project

178 In der nächsten Aufgabe sollst du einen Dialog über das *Eden Project* schreiben. Bevor du damit beginnst, übe hier, wie man Fragen stellt und dazu passende Antworten gibt.

a) "What are you doing?"
"I _____ *(schauen)* at the Eden Project on the internet."

b) "_____?"
"Yes, I'm on holiday here. I come from Germany."

c) "Are you having a nice holiday in Cornwall?"
"_____. Thank _____."

179 Schaue dir die Fotos vom *Eden Project* an.
Vervollständige den Dialog auf der nächsten Seite.

Topic 45: The Eden Project

a) TOM: *(fragt Sally, wo das Eden Project ist)*

   _____

   SALLY: It's in Cornwall, England.

b) TOM: *(will wissen, was das Eden Project ist)*

   _____

   SALLY: It is a project about us, the climate and plants – a 'global garden'.

   TOM: *(fragt, was die verschiedenen Klimazonen sind)*

   _____

   SALLY: There are three – there is a Mediterranean dome *(Mittelmeer-Kuppel)* and a rainforest *(Regenwald)* dome, then outside there is the normal climate for Cornwall.

   TOM: *(fragt, was in den Kuppeln ist)*

   _____

   SALLY: Flowers, plants, bananas and lots of other things – the rainforest dome is very hot.

c) TOM: *(fragt nach dem Eintrittspreis)*

   _____

   SALLY: £ 16 for adults and £ 5 for children.

   TOM: *(möchte wissen, wann es offen ist)*

   _____

   SALLY: In summer, from 10 a.m. to 6 p.m.

180 Im *Eden Project* gibt es eine Pinnwand, an der du Informationen über dein eigenes Leben aufhängen kannst. Forscher können dann herausfinden, wie wir alle leben. Fülle das Formular aus.

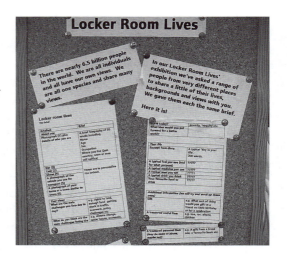

YOU

Draw yourself (or: photo of you).

Write about yourself.
(Your name, age, where you come from, what you like doing, …)

_____
_____
_____
_____

Draw how you usually travel (or photo).

Draw your home (or photo).

What is a typical day for you? _____
_____
_____

What is your favourite food? _____
What is your favourite drink? _____
What is your favourite thing? _____

Vocabulary –
Vokabelverzeichnis

Nicht alle in diesem Buch verwendeten Wörter stehen in der Vokabelliste, z. B. Wochen- und Monatsnamen, Zahlen, Personalpronomen, *a, an, the* oder *to be* solltest du kennen, bzw. du kannst sie im Vokabelverzeichnis deines Englischbuches nachschlagen.

Englisch – Deutsch

a lot of	– viele	animal	– Tier
about	– über, ungefähr	another	– noch einer, ein anderer
across	– über		
address	– Adresse	(to) answer	– antworten
admission	– Eintritt(spreis)	answer	– Antwort
adult	– Erwachsene(r)	any	– irgend-
adventure playground	– Abenteuerspielplatz	anybody	– jeder, irgendeiner
		anywhere	– irgendwo, überall
Africa	– Afrika	area	– Gebiet
after	– nach	arm	– Arm
after that	– danach	armchair	– Sessel
afternoon	– Nachmittag	around	– um (…) herum
again	– nochmals, wieder	(to) arrive	– ankommen
ago	– vor	as	– als, wie
airport	– Flughafen	(to) ask	– fragen
all	– alle	at	– an, um *(Uhrzeit)*
all day	– den ganzen Tag	at the moment	– im Augenblick
almost	– fast	attention	– Achtung
along	– entlang	aunt	– Tante
also	– auch	(far) away	– (weit) weg
always	– immer		
America	– Amerika	baby	– Baby
American	– Amerikaner, amerikanisch	back	– Rücken, zurück, Rückseite
and	– und	bad	– schlecht
angry	– böse		

Vocabulary

badge	– Abzeichen, Button	body	– Körper
bag	– Tasche	(to) book	– buchen
bagel	– Bagel *(ringförmiges Gebäck)*	book	– Buch
		bookshelf	– Bücherregal
		bookshop	– Buchladen
baguette	– Baguette	boring	– langweilig
baker	– Bäcker(in)	both	– beide
balcony	– Balkon	bowl	– Schüssel
ball	– Ball	box	– Kiste
banana	– Banane	boy	– Junge
band	– Band	bread	– Brot
(to) bang	– knallen, zuschlagen	(to) break	– brechen
		breakfast	– Frühstück
bank	– Bank	bridge	– Brücke
baseball	– Baseball	(to) bring	– bringen
bathroom	– Badezimmer	Britain	– Großbritannien
battle	– Schlacht	British	– britisch
beach	– Strand	broken	– gebrochen
bear	– Bär	brother	– Bruder
beautiful	– wunderschön	brown	– braun
because	– weil	(to) brush	– bürsten
bed	– Bett	building	– Gebäude
bedroom	– Schlafzimmer	bus	– Bus
before	– vor	bus station	– Busbahnhof
(to) begin	– anfangen	bus stop	– Bushaltestelle
behind	– hinter	bush	– Busch
better	– besser	but	– aber
between	– zwischen	(to) buy	– kaufen
big	– groß	by	– von
bike	– Fahrrad	by (car, train)	– mit (dem Auto, dem Zug)
bird	– Vogel		
birthday	– Geburtstag	bye	– Tschüs
black	– schwarz		
(black)board	– Tafel	café	– Café
blonde	– blond	cake	– Kuchen
blouse	– Bluse	(to be) called	– heißen
blue	– blau	camera	– Kamera
boarding pass	– Bordkarte	(to) catch a bus	– den Bus bekommen / nehmen
boat	– Boot		

caution	– Vorsicht	country	– Land
cell phone	– Handy	countryside	– Land, Landschaft
centre (B.E.), center (A.E.)	– Zentrum, Mitte	cousin	– Cousin(e)
		cow	– Kuh
chair	– Stuhl	cup	– Tasse
(to) chase	– jagen, hinter jmd. / etw. herlaufen	cupboard	– Schrank
		(to) cut	– schneiden
(to) chat	– chatten	(to) cycle	– Rad fahren
chest	– Brust		
child (children)	– Kind (Kinder)	dad	– Papa, Vati
chimney	– Schornstein	daily	– täglich
chips	– Pommes frites	(to) dance	– tanzen
church	– Kirche	dark	– dunkel
cinema	– Kino	date	– Datum
city	– Großstadt	daughter	– Tochter
class	– Klasse	day	– Tag
classroom	– Klassenzimmer	Dear (John)	– Lieber (John)
(to) clean	– putzen	(to) deliver (newspapers)	– (Zeitungen) austragen
clever	– klug, schlau		
climate	– Klima	(to) describe	– beschreiben
(to) climb	– klettern	desert island	– einsame Insel
(to) close	– schließen	desk	– Schreibtisch
clothes	– Kleidung	dessert	– Nachtisch
coast	– Küste	details	– Details, Angaben
coat	– Mantel	(to) dial	– wählen
coffee	– Kaffee	different(ly)	– verschieden, anders
cold	– kalt, Erkältung		
(to) collect	– sammeln, abholen	difficult	– schwer, schwierig
		dining room	– Esszimmer
colour (B.E.), color (A.E.)	– Farbe	dinner	– Essen, Hauptmahlzeit
(to) come	– kommen	dinosaur	– Dinosaurier
(to) come from	– kommen aus	dirt	– Schmutz, Dreck
come on	– Komm!	(to) discover	– entdecken
comma	– Komma	(to) do	– machen
computer	– Computer	doctor	– Arzt, Ärztin
concert	– Konzert	dog	– Hund
(to) cost	– kosten	dome	– Kuppel
could	– konnte, könnte	door	– Tür

doorbell	– Türklingel	expensive	– teuer
doorstep	– Türschwelle	eye	– Auge
(to) download	– herunterladen		
downstairs	– (nach) unten	(not) fair	– (un)fair
(to) draw	– zeichnen	false	– falsch
dress	– Kleid	family	– Familie
(to) drink	– trinken	famous	– berühmt
drink	– Getränk	fantasy	– Fantasie
(to) drive	– fahren	far (away)	– weit (weg)
drive	– Auffahrt	farm	– Bauernhof
		farmer	– Bauer, Bäuerin
each	– jeder/-e/-s	fast	– schnell
each other	– einander	fat	– dick
early	– früh	father	– Vater
easy	– leicht, einfach	favourite	– Lieblings-
(to) eat	– essen	(to) feed	– füttern
egg	– Ei	(to) feel ill	– (sich) krank
elephant	– Elefant		(fühlen)
e-mail	– E-Mail	felt pen	– Filzstift
embarrassing	– peinlich	fence	– Zaun
end	– Ende	(to) find	– finden
England	– England	fine	– (hier) gut
English	– englisch,	finger	– Finger
	Engländer(in)	(to) finish	– (be)enden
(to) enjoy	– genießen	fire	– Feuer
enough	– genug, genügend	first	– erste/-r/-s
(to) enter	– hineingehen	fish	– Fisch
evening	– Abend	flat	– Wohnung
every	– jeder/-e/-s	flower	– Blume
everybody,	– jeder/-e/-s	(to) fly	– fliegen
everyone		foal	– Fohlen
everything	– alles	food	– Lebensmittel
everywhere	– überall	foot (feet)	– Fuß (Füße)
exactly	– genau	football	– Fußball
example	– Beispiel	football team	– Fußball-
exclamation	– Ausrufezeichen		mannschaft
mark		footballer	– Fußballspieler(in)
excuse me	– Entschuldigung	footprint	– Fußabdruck
		for	– für

for example	– zum Beispiel	girl	– Mädchen
forest	– Forst, Wald	(to) give	– geben
(to) forget	– vergessen	glass	– Glas
fork	– Gabel	glasses	– Brille
form	– Formular	gloves	– Handschuhe
free	– kostenlos	(to) go	– gehen
free time	– Freizeit	(to) go by	– fahren mit
friend	– Freund	(to) go into	– hineingehen
friendly	– freundlich	(to) go on	– weitergehen
fries (A.E.)	– Pommes frites	(to) go past	– vorbeigehen
(to be) frightened	– Angst haben	(to be) going to	– werden
		gold	– Gold
frog	– Frosch	good	– gut
from	– von, aus	good luck	– viel Glück
from (6.30)	– ab (6.30)	goodbye	– auf Wiedersehen
front door	– Haustür	gram	– Gramm
fruit	– Obst	grandad	– Opa
full stop	– Punkt	grandma	– Oma
fun	– Spaß	grandparents	– Großeltern
fun park	– Freizeitpark	grass	– Gras
fun-run	– Wohltätigkeits-lauf	great	– toll, fantastisch
		green	– grün
funny	– witzig, lustig	grey	– grau
		group	– Gruppe
game	– Spiel		
garage	– Garage	hair	– Haar(e)
garden	– Garten	half	– halb
gate	– Tor, Gate	half past (three)	– halb (vier)
Germany	– Deutschland	half price	– halber Preis
(to) get	– bekommen	hall	– Saal, Diele, Flur
(to) get in(to)	– einsteigen	(Holkham) Hall	– Herrenhaus
(to) get off	– aus-/absteigen	hand	– Hand
(to) get on(to)	– ein-/aufsteigen	(to) happen	– passieren
(to) get out of	– aussteigen aus	happy	– glücklich
(to) get ready	– sich fertig machen	happy birthday	– Herzlichen Glückwunsch zum Geburtstag
(to) get to	– kommen zu		
ghost	– Geist, Gespenst	harbour (B.E.), harbor (A.E.)	– Hafen
ghost train	– Geisterbahn		

has / have	– haben	(to) hurt	– wehtun, schmerzen
has / have got	– haben, besitzen		
hat	– Mütze, Hut	husband	– Ehemann
(to) hate	– hassen		
(to) have to	– müssen	ice	– Eiswürfel
head	– Kopf	ice cream	– Eis
headache	– Kopfschmerzen	idea	– Idee
heading	– Überschrift	if	– wenn, falls, ob
(to) hear	– hören	ill	– krank
heavy	– schwer	illness	– Krankheit
hedge	– Hecke	in front of	– vor
hello	– hallo	Indian	– Indianer
helmet	– Helm	information	– Information
(to) help	– helfen	inside	– innen
her	– sie, ihr	interesting	– interessant
here	– hier	internet	– Internet
hi	– hallo	into	– in, hinein
hill	– Hügel	(to) invite	– einladen
him	– ihm, ihn	island	– Insel
his	– sein		
historic	– historisch	jacket	– Jacke
(to) hit (a ball)	– schlagen, treffen	(a pair of) jeans	– Jeans
(to) hold	– (fest)halten	jewellery (B.E.), jewelry (A.E.)	– Schmuck
holiday	– Urlaub, Ferien		
home	– zu Hause	job	– Beruf
homework	– Hausaufgaben	(to) jog	– joggen
(to) hope	– hoffen	joke	– Witz
horrible	– schrecklich	July	– Juli
horse	– Pferd	(to) jump	– springen
horse riding	– reiten	just	– nur, bloß
hot	– heiß		
(an) hour	– (eine) Stunde	kangaroo	– Känguru
house	– Haus	kilometre	– Kilometer
how?	– wie?	kilt	– Schottenrock
how many?	– wie viele?	king	– König
how much?	– wie viel?	kitchen	– Küche
how old?	– wie alt?	kitten	– Kätzchen
hump	– Buckel	knee	– Knie
(to be) hungry	– Hunger (haben)		

knife	– Messer	(to) lose	– verlieren
(to) know	– wissen, kennen	(a) lot of	– viel(e)
		loud	– laut
lake	– See	love	– Grüße
lamb	– Lamm	lovely	– schön, herrlich
lamp	– Lampe	lucky	– glücklich
land	– Land, Boden	lunch	– Mittagessen
landing	– Treppenabsatz, Flur		
		made of	– aus
large	– groß	main street/ road	– Hauptstraße
last	– letzte/-r/-s		
(to be) late	– spät	(to) make	– machen
(to) laugh	– lachen	man (men)	– Mann (Männer)
lead	– Leine	many	– viele
(to) leave	– verlassen, abreisen	market place	– Markt(platz)
		married	– verheiratet
left	– links	mask	– Maske
leg	– Bein	Maths	– Mathe(matik)
lesson	– Unterricht (sstunde)	maybe	– vielleicht
		me	– mich, mir
let's	– lass/lasst uns	meal	– Mahlzeit
letter	– Brief, Buchstaben	(to) mean	– bedeuten
light	– Licht, Lampe	meat	– Fleisch
like	– wie	(to) meet	– treffen
(to) like	– mögen, gefallen	message	– Nachricht
lion	– Löwe	metre	– Meter
list	– Liste	microphone	– Mikrofon
(to) listen to	– (zu)hören	middle	– mittlere/-r/-s
(to) live	– wohnen, leben	(in the) middle	– in der Mitte
live music	– Livemusik	mile	– Meile
living room	– Wohnzimmer	(to) milk	– melken
loch	– (See in Schottland)	million	– Million
		mine	– meine/-r/-s
long	– lang	minute	– Minute
(to) look	– sehen, schauen	(to) miss	– verpassen
(to) look at	– ansehen	missing	– verschwunden, fehlend(e)
(to) look for	– suchen nach		
(to) look out of	– herausschauen	mobile (phone)	– Handy
lorry	– Lastwagen	money	– Geld

monkey	– Affe
monster	– Monster
month	– Monat
more	– mehr
morning	– Morgen
most	– die meisten
mother	– Mutter
motorbike	– Motorrad
mountain biking	– Mountainbike fahren
mouse (mice)	– Maus (Mäuse)
mum	– Mutti, Mama
museum	– Museum
music	– Musik
must	– müssen
my	– meine/-r/-s
name	– Name
Native American	– amerikanischer Ureinwohner
near	– nahe, in der Nähe von
neck	– Hals
(to) need	– brauchen, benötigen
neighbour (B.E.) neighbor (A.E.)	– Nachbar
nephew	– Neffe
never	– nie
new	– neu
newspaper	– Zeitung
next	– nächste/-r/-s
next to	– neben
nice	– schön
night	– Nacht
no	– nein, kein
no one	– niemand
nobody	– niemand, keiner
noise	– Lärm, Geräusch
noon	– Mittag
no problem	– kein Problem
normal	– normal
north of	– nördlich von
not	– nicht
not (…) at all	– überhaupt nicht
notes	– Notizen
nothing	– nichts
notice board	– Aushang, schwarzes Brett
now	– jetzt
nowhere	– nirgendwo
number	– Nummer, Zahl
(3) o'clock	– (3) Uhr
object	– Sache, Ding
of	– von
of course	– natürlich
official	– offiziell
often	– oft
old	– alt
on	– auf, an (mit Dativ)
on the right/left	– auf der rechten/linken Seite
one way ticket	– einfache Fahrkarte
only	– nur
(the) only	– der/die/das Einzige
onto	– auf (mit Akk.)
(to) open	– öffnen
opening times	– Öffnungszeiten
opposite	– gegenüber
or	– oder
orange	– orange
(the) other	– der/die/das andere
others	– andere
outside	– außen, draußen

over	– über	planet	– Planet
over there	– dort hinüber, dort drüben	plant	– Pflanze
		plate	– Teller
		platform	– Bahnsteig
Pacific coast	– Pazifikküste	(to) play	– spielen
(to) paint	– malen	playground	– Spielplatz
paintbrush	– Pinsel	please	– bitte
palm tree	– Palme	plum	– Pflaume
panini	– Panini *(ital. Sandwich)*	polar bear	– Eisbär
		police	– Polizei
parents	– Eltern	pond	– Teich
(to) park	– parken	poor	– arm
park	– Park	pop group	– Popgruppe
part	– Teil	possible	– möglich
partner	– Partner	potato	– Kartoffel
party	– Party	present	– Geschenk
(to) pass (by)	– vorbeigehen	(to) press	– drücken
passenger	– Reisende(r)	pretty	– hübsch
path	– Weg	price	– Preis
pavement	– Bürgersteig	probably	– wahrscheinlich
pelican	– Pelikan	problem	– Problem
pen	– Füller	profile	– Profil
pencil	– Bleistift	programme	– Sendung
pencil case	– Federmäppchen	project	– Projekt
pencil crayon	– Buntstift	pullover	– Pullover
people	– Leute, Menschen	pupil	– Schüler(in)
pet	– Haustier	puppy	– Welpe
(to) phone	– anrufen	(to) purchase	– kaufen
photo(graph)	– Foto, Fotografie	purple	– lila, violett
(to) pick (flowers)	– (Blumen) pflücken	(to) push	– schieben
		(to) put	– setzen, stellen, legen
(to) pick up	– abholen		
picture	– Bild		
piece of paper	– Blatt Papier	(a) quarter (past/to)	– Viertel (nach/vor)
pig	– Schwein		
pilot	– Pilot(in)	question	– Frage
pink	– Pink	question mark	– Fragezeichen
place	– Ort, Platz	quick(ly)	– schnell
plane	– Flugzeug	quiet	– leise, ruhig

radio	– Radio	sand	– Sand
(to) rain	– regnen	sandwich	– Sandwich
rain	– Regen	Santa Claus	– Weihnachtsmann
rainforest	– Regenwald	saucer	– Untertasse
(to) read	– lesen	(to) save	– (hier) retten
ready	– fertig	(to) say	– sagen
real	– echt	scarf	– Schal
really	– wirklich	scary	– Furcht erregend
receptionist	– Personal am Empfang (Hotel)	school	– Schule
		school field	– Schulsportplatz
red	– rot	school uniform	– Schuluniform
(to) remember	– sich erinnern	schoolbag	– Schultasche
reservation	– Reservierung	scissors	– Schere
restaurant	– Restaurant	scorpion	– Skorpion
rich	– reich	Scotland	– Schottland
(to) ride	– fahren, reiten	Scotsman	– Schotte
right	– rechts, richtig	sea	– Meer
(to) ring	– klingeln	seal	– Robbe
river	– Fluss	second	– zweite/-r/-s
road	– Straße	(to) see	– sehen
robber	– Räuber	(to) sell	– verkaufen
(to) rollerblade	– inlineskaten	(to) send	– schicken
roof	– Dach	sentence	– Satz
room	– Zimmer	shed	– Schuppen
rose	– Rose	sheep	– Schaf
row	– Reihe	shelf (shelves)	– Regal
rubber	– Radiergummi	shirt	– Hemd
ruler	– Lineal	shoe	– Schuh
(to) run	– laufen	shop	– Laden, Geschäft
(to) run away	– weglaufen	shopping	– Einkaufen
		short	– kurz
sad	– traurig	(a pair of) shorts	– kurze Hose, Shorts
safe	– sicher		
saint	– Sankt, Heiliger	(to) shout	– schreien
salad	– Salat	side	– Seite
sale	– Schlussverkauf	sidewalk (A.E.)	– Bürgersteig
(on) sale	– zu verkaufen	sign	– Schild
(the) same	– der/die/das gleiche	signpost	– Wegweiser

sights	– Sehenswürdigkeiten	(to) stand	– stehen
(to) sing	– singen	(to) start	– beginnen
single	– ledig	station	– Bahnhof
sister	– Schwester	(to) stay	– bleiben, übernachten
(to) sit	– sitzen	step up	– steigern, verbessern
size	– Größe		
skateboard	– Skateboard	still	– noch
(to) skateboard	– Skateboard fahren	stone	– Stein
		(to) stop	– anhalten
skeleton	– Skelett	story	– Geschichte
skirt	– Rock	strange	– seltsam
sky	– Himmel	street	– Straße
(to) sleep	– schlafen	stripe	– Streifen
slow	– langsam	studio	– Studio
small(er)	– klein(er)	suddenly	– plötzlich
(to) snow	– schneien	suitcase	– Koffer
so	– so	summer	– Sommer
(a pair of) socks	– Socken, Kniestrümpfe	sun	– Sonne
		sunny	– sonnig
sofa	– Sofa, Couch	super	– super, klasse, fantastisch
some	– irgendein, einige		
somebody	– jemand	supermarket	– Supermarkt
something	– etwas	sure	– (hier) natürlich
sometimes	– manchmal	surface	– Oberfläche
somewhere	– irgendwo	surfing	– Surfen
son	– Sohn	surprise	– Überraschung
song	– Lied	sweatshirt	– Sweatshirt
sore	– entzündet, schmerzhaft	(to) swim	– schwimmen
		swimming pool	– Schwimmbecken
sorry	– es tut mir leid	swollen	– geschwollen
soup	– Suppe	sword	– Schwert
south/South	– südlich, Süden		
(to) speak	– reden	table	– Tisch
(to) spell	– buchstabieren	(to) take	– (mit)nehmen
spoon	– Löffel	(to) take a photo	– ein Foto machen
staff	– Mitarbeiter, Belegschaft		
		(to) take away	– mitnehmen
stairs	– Treppe	(to) talk (to)	– sprechen (mit)

tall	– groß	together	– zusammen
tea	– Tee	toilet	– Toilette
(to) teach	– unterrichten	tomato	– Tomate
teacher	– Lehrer(in)	tomorrow	– morgen
team	– Mannschaft	tonight	– heute Abend
teddy bear	– Teddybär	too	– auch
teenager	– Teenager	toothache	– Zahnschmerzen
television	– Fernsehen	top	– oben
(to) tell	– erzählen	tour	– Tour, Rundreise
tennis	– Tennis	tourist	– Tourist(in)
terrible	– schrecklich	towards	– auf (…) zu
text	– Text	tower	– Turm
(to) text	– eine SMS schreiben/senden	town	– Stadt
		town centre	– Stadtzentrum
thank you (thanks)	– danke	traffic lights	– Ampel
		train	– Zug
that	– diese/-r/-s, dass	training shoes (trainers)	– Sportschuhe
their	– ihr		
them	– sie, ihnen	(to) travel	– reisen
then	– dann, damals	tree	– Baum
there is/are	– es gibt, dort sind, dort ist	(a pair of) trousers	– Hose
these	– diese	(to) try on	– anprobieren
thing	– Ding, Sache	T-shirt	– T-Shirt
(to) think	– glauben, denken	(to) turn (left/right)	– (links/rechts) abbiegen
this	– diese/-r/-s		
those	– jene	type	– Art
through	– durch	typical	– typisch
(to) throw	– werfen		
thumb	– Daumen	umbrella	– Regenschirm
ticket	– Fahrkarte, Eintrittskarte	uncle	– Onkel
		under	– unter
ticket office	– Fahrkartenschalter, Kasse	(to) understand	– verstehen
		uneven	– uneben, holprig
tie	– Krawatte	unhappy	– unglücklich
time	– Zeit, Mal	uniform	– Uniform
title	– Titel	until	– bis
to	– zu, nach	unusual	– ungewöhnlich
today	– heute	upstairs	– oben

us	– uns	which?	– welche/-r/-s?
(to) use	– (be)nutzen	white	– weiß
usually	– gewöhnlich	who?	– wer?
		whose?	– wessen?
van	– Lieferwagen	why?	– warum?
very	– sehr	wife	– Ehefrau
view	– Aussicht	wildlife park	– Wildpark
village	– Dorf	will	– werden
(to) visit	– besuchen	window	– Fenster
voice	– Stimme	windy	– windig
volleyball	– Volleyball	winter	– Winter
		with	– mit, dabei
(to) **w**ait	– warten	without	– ohne
(to) wake up	– aufwachen	woman	– Frau
(to) walk	– (zu Fuß) gehen	wood	– Holz
walk	– Spaziergang	word	– Wort
wall	– Wand	(to) work	– arbeiten
(to) want (to)	– wollen	work	– Arbeit
wardrobe	– Kleiderschrank	wow!	– toll!, Wahnsinn!,
warm	– warm		super!
wash	– Wäsche	(to) write	– schreiben
(to) wash	– waschen	wrong	– falsch
(to) watch	– ansehen, zusehen		
water	– Wasser	**y**ear	– Jahr
wave	– Welle	(…) years old	– (…) Jahre alt
(to) wear	– tragen	yellow	– gelb
weather	– Wetter	yes	– ja
weather report	– Wetterbericht	your	– dein, euer, Ihr
week	– Woche	yourself	– dich, dir selbst
weekend	– Wochenende	young	– jung
welcome	– Willkommen		
wet	– nass		
what?	– was?		
	welche/-r/-s?		
what about?	– was ist mit?		
what's wrong?	– was ist los?		
what time?	– wie viel Uhr?		
when?	– wann?		
where?	– wo?		

Deutsch–English

ab (6.30)	– from (6.30)
(links/rechts) abbiegen	– (to) turn (left/right)
Abend	– evening
Abenteuerspielplatz	– adventure playground
aber	– but
Abfahrt	– departure
abholen	– (to) pick up
Adresse	– address
Affe	– monkey
Afrika	– Africa
alle	– all
alles	– everything
als, wie	– as
alt	– old
Alter	– age
Amerika	– America
Ampel	– traffic lights
anbieten	– (to) offer
andere	– others
anfangen	– (to) begin
Angst haben	– (to be) frightened
anhalten	– (to) stop
ankommen	– (to) arrive
anprobieren	– (to) try on
anrufen	– (to) phone
ansehen	– (to) look at, (to) watch
Antwort	– answer
antworten	– (to) answer
Arbeit	– work
arbeiten	– (to) work
Arm	– arm
arm	– poor
Art	– type
Arzt, Ärztin	– doctor
auch	– also, too
auf (mit Akk.)	– onto
auf / an (mit Dativ)	– on
auf Wiedersehen	– goodbye
auf (...) zu	– towards
Auffahrt	– drive
aufregend	– exciting
aufwachen	– (to) wake up
Auge	– eye
aus	– made of
Ausgang	– exit
Ausland	– abroad
Ausrufezeichen	– exclamation mark
außen	– outside
aussteigen	– (to) get off
aussteigen aus	– (to) get out of
Auswahl	– choice
Auto	– car
Baby	– baby
Bäcker(in)	– baker
Badezimmer	– bathroom
Bagel	– bagel
Baguette	– baguette
Bahnhof	– station
Bahnsteig	– platform
Bahnübergang	– level crossing
Balkon	– balcony
Ball	– ball
Banane	– banana
Band	– band
Bank	– bank
Bär	– bear
Baseball	– baseball

Bauer/Bäuerin	– farmer	Brot	– bread
Bauernhof	– farm	Brücke	– bridge
Baum	– tree	Bruder	– brother
bedeuten	– (to) mean	Brust	– chest
beenden	– (to) finish	Buch	– book
begehbar	– to be open	buchen	– (to) book
beginnen	– (to) start	Bücherregal	– bookshelf
Bein	– leg	Buckel	– hump
Beispiel	– example	Buntstift	– pencil crayon
bekommen	– (to) get	Bürgersteig	– pavement (B.E.), sidewalk (A.E.)
benutzen	– (to) use		
Beruf	– job	bürsten	– (to) brush
berühmt	– famous	Bus	– bus
beschreiben	– (to) describe	Busbahnhof	– bus station
Beschreibung	– description	Busch	– bush
besitzen	– have/has got	Bushaltestelle	– bus stop
besser	– better		
besuchen	– (to) visit	Café	– café
Bett	– bed	chatten	– (to) chat
Bild	– picture	Clown	– clown
bis	– until	Computer	– computer
bitte	– please	Cousin(e)	– cousin
Blatt Papier	– piece of paper		
blau	– blue	Dach	– roof
bleiben	– (to) stay	danach	– after that
Bleistift	– pencil	danke	– thank you (thanks)
blond	– blonde		
Blume	– flower	dann, damals	– then
Bluse	– blouse	Datum	– date
Boot	– boat	dauern	– (to) last
Bordkarte	– boarding pass	Daumen	– thumb
böse	– angry	dein, euer, Ihr	– your
brauchen	– (to) need	denken	– (to) think
braun	– brown	der/die/das andere	– (the) other
brechen	– (to) break		
Brief, Buchstaben	– letter	der/die/das einzige	– (the) only
Brille	– glasses	der/die/das gleiche	– (the) same
bringen	– (to) bring		

deshalb	– therefore
Details	– details
Deutschland	– Germany
dich, dir selbst	– yourself
die meisten	– most
diese	– these
diese/-r/-s	– this
diese/-r/-s, dass	– that
Ding	– thing
Dorf	– village
dort hinüber, dort drüben	– over there
dunkel	– dark
durch	– through
dürfen	– may
echt	– real
Ehefrau	– wife
Ehemann	– husband
ein, eine	– a (an)
Einkaufen	– shopping
einladen	– (to) invite
einsam	– lonely
einsame Insel	– desert island
einsteigen	– (to) get in, into
einsteigen, aufsteigen	– (to) get on/onto
Eintrittskarte	– ticket
Eintritt(spreis)	– admission
Eis	– ice cream
Eisbär	– polar bear
Eiswürfel	– ice (cube)
Elefant	– elephant
Eltern	– parents
E-Mail	– e-mail
Ende	– end
England	– England
englisch, Engländer(in)	– English
entdecken	– (to) discover
entlang	– along
entzündet	– sore
Erkältung	– cold
erste/-r/-es	– first
Erwachsene(r)	– adult
erzählen	– (to) tell
es gibt	– there is/are
es tut mir leid	– sorry
essen	– (to) eat
(Abend-)Essen	– dinner
Esszimmer	– dining room
etwas	– something
Fahrbahn	– road
fahren	– (to) drive, (to) ride
fahren mit	– (to) go by
Fahrgast	– passenger
Fahrkarte	– ticket
Fahrrad	– bike
Fahrrad fahren	– (to) cycle
fair	– fair
falsch	– wrong, false
Familie	– family
Farbe	– colour (B.E.), color (A.E.)
faul	– (to be) lazy
Federmäppchen	– pencil case
Fenster	– window
Fernsehen	– television
fertig	– ready
(sich) fertig machen	– (to) get ready
festhalten	– (to) hold
Feuer	– fire
Filzstift	– felt pen

finden	– (to) find	gebrochen	– broken
Finger	– finger	Geburtstag	– birthday
Fisch	– fish	Gegenteil	– opposite
Fleisch	– meat	gegenüber	– opposite
fliegen	– (to) fly	gehen	– (to) go
Flughafen	– airport	(zu Fuß) gehen	– (to) walk
Flugzeug	– plane	Geist, Gespenst	– ghost
Fluss	– river	Geisterbahn	– ghost train
Fohlen	– foal	gelb	– yellow
Foto	– photo(graph)	Geld	– money
Foto machen	– (to) take a photo	genießen	– (to) enjoy
Frage	– question	genug	– enough
fragen	– (to) ask	gerade	– at the moment
Fragezeichen	– question mark	geradeaus	– straight forward
Frau	– woman	Geschäft	– shop, business
Freizeit	– free time	Geschenk	– present
Freizeitpark	– fun park	Geschichte	– story
Freund	– friend	geschwollen	– swollen
fröhlich	– happy, cheerful	Getränk	– drink
Frosch	– frog	gewöhnlich	– usually
früh	– early	Glas	– glass
Frühstück	– breakfast	glauben	– (to) think
Füller	– pen	glücklich	– happy, lucky
für	– for	Gold	– gold
furchterregend	– scary	Gramm	– gram
Fuß (Füße)	– foot (feet)	Gras	– grass
Fußball	– football	grau	– grey
Fußball-mannschaft	– football team	groß	– big, large, tall
		Größe	– size
Fußball-spieler(in)	– footballer	Großeltern	– grandparents
		Großstadt	– city
füttern	– (to) feed	grün	– green
		Gruppe	– group
Gabel	– fork	Grüße	– love
Garage	– garage	gut	– good
Garten	– garden		
Gebäude	– building		
geben	– (to) give		
Gebiet	– area		

Haar(e)	– hair
haben	– has/have got
Hafen	– harbour (B.E.), harbour (A.E.)
Hafenrundfahrt	– harbour tour
halb	– half
halb (vier)	– half past (three)
halber Preis	– half price
hallo	– hello, hi
Hals	– neck
halten	– (to) hold
Hand	– hand
Handschuhe	– (a pair of) gloves
Handy	– mobile (phone), cell phone (A.E.)
hassen	– (to) hate
Hauptstraße	– main street/road
Haus	– house
Hausaufgaben	– homework
Haustier	– pet
Haustür	– front door
Hecke	– hedge
heiß	– hot
heißen	– (to be) called
helfen	– (to) help
Helm	– helmet
Hemd	– shirt
herausschauen	– (to) look out of
Herrenhaus	– (Holkham) Hall
Herzlichen Glückwunsch zum Geburtstag	– happy birthday
heute	– today
heute Abend	– tonight
hier	– here
Himmel	– sky
hineinbringen	– (to) bring in, (to) take into
hineingehen	– (to) enter, (to) go into
hineinwachsen	– (to) grow into
hinter	– behind
hinter jmd./etw. herlaufen	– (to) chase
hoffen	– (to) hope
Holz	– wood
hören	– (to) hear
(zu)hören	– (to) listen
Hose	– (a pair of) trousers
Hügel	– hill
Hund	– dog
Hunger (haben)	– (to be) hungry
Idee	– idea
ihm, ihn	– him
ihr	– her, their
im Augenblick	– at the moment
immer	– always
in	– in
in der Mitte	– (in the) middle
in, hinein	– into
in Richtung	– in the direction of
Information	– information
innen	– inside
Insekt	– insect
Insel	– island
interessant	– interesting
Internet	– internet
irgendein	– some
irgendwo	– anywhere
Irisch	– Irish
ja	– yes
Jacke	– jacket
Jahr	– year
(…) Jahre alt	– (…) years old

Jeans	– (a pair of) jeans	kommen aus	– (to) come from
jede/-r/-s	– each, every, any	kommen zu	– (to) get to
jeder	– everyone	König	– king
jemand	– somebody	konnte, könnte	– could
jene	– those	Konzert	– concert
jetzt	– now	Kopf	– head
Jubiläum	– anniversary	Kopfschmerzen	– headache
jung	– young	Körper	– body
Junge	– boy	kosten	– (to) cost
		kostenlos	– free
Kaffee	– coffee	krank	– ill
kalt	– cold	(sich) krank (fühlen)	– (to) feel ill
Kamera	– camera		
Känguru	– kangaroo	Krankheit	– illness
kann, können	– can	Krawatte	– tie
Kartoffel	– potato	Küche	– kitchen
Kätzchen	– kitten	Kuchen	– cake
Katze	– cat	Kuh	– cow
kaufen	– (to) buy	Kuppel	– dome
kein Problem	– no problem	kurz	– short
Kilometer	– kilometre	kurze Hose	– (a pair of) shorts
Kind (Kinder)	– child (children)		
Kino	– cinema	lächeln	– (to) smile
Kiste	– box	lachen	– (to) laugh
Klassenzimmer	– classroom	Laden	– shop
Kleid	– dress	Lamm	– lamb
Kleiderschrank	– wardrobe	Lampe	– lamp
Kleidung	– clothes	Land	– country
klein(er)	– small(er)	Land, Boden	– land
Klima	– climate	lang	– long
klingeln	– (to) ring	Langlauf	– cross-country skiing
klingt gut	– sounds good		
klug	– clever	langsam	– slow
knallen	– (to) bang	langweilig	– boring
Knie	– knee	Lärm	– noise
Knochen	– bone	lass/lasst uns	– let's
komm	– come on	Lastwagen	– lorry
Komma	– comma	laufen	– (to) run
kommen	– (to) come	laut	– loud

Leben	– life	Mathe(matik)	– Maths
Lebensmittel	– food	Maus (Mäuse)	– mouse (mice)
ledig	– single	Mechaniker(in)	– mechanic
Lehrer(in)	– teacher	Meer	– sea
leicht	– easy	mehr	– more
leider	– unfortunately	Meile	– mile
Leine	– lead	mein	– my
leise	– quiet	meine/-r/-s	– mine
lesen	– (to) read	melken	– (to) milk
letzte/-r/-s	– last	merkwürdig	– strange
Leute	– people	Messer	– knife
Licht	– light	Meter	– metre
lieben	– (to) love	mich / mir	– me
Lieber (John)	– Dear (John)	Mikrofon	– microphone
Lieblings-	– favourite	Minute	– minute
Lied	– song	mit (dem Auto/Zug)	– by (car / train)
Lieferwagen	– van		
lila	– purple	mit, dabei	– with
Lineal	– ruler	Mitarbeiter	– staff
links	– left	mitnehmen	– (to) take away
Liste	– list	Mittag	– noon
Livemusik	– live music	Mittagessen	– lunch
Löffel	– spoon	Mittelmeer	– (the) Mediterranean
Löwe	– lion		
lustig	– funny	mittlere/-r/-s	– middle
		mögen	– (to) like
machen	– (to) do, (to) make	möglich	– possible
Mädchen	– girl	Monat	– month
Mahlzeit	– meal	Monster	– monster
malen	– (to) paint	Morgen	– morning
Maler(in)	– painter	Motorrad	– motorbike
man	– one	Mountainbike fahren	– mountain biking
manchmal	– sometimes		
Mann (Männer)	– man (men)	Museum	– museum
Mannschaft	– team	Musik	– music
Mantel	– coat	müssen	– (to) have to, must
Markt	– market	Mutter	– mother
Marktplatz	– market place	Mutti, Mama	– mum
Maske	– mask	Mütze	– cap, hat

nach	– after	oft	– often
Nachbar(in)	– neighbour (B.E.), neighbor (A.E.)	ohne	– without
		Oma	– grandma
Nachfolger	– successor	Onkel	– uncle
Nachmittag	– afternoon	Opa	– grandad
Nachricht	– message	orange	– orange
Nachrichten	– news	Ort	– place
nächste/-r/-s	– next		
Nacht	– night	**P**addeln	– canoeing
Nachtisch	– dessert	Panini *(ital.*	– panini
nahe	– near	*Sandwich)*	
Name	– name	Papa	– dad
nass	– wet	Park	– park
natürlich	– of course	parken	– (to) park
neben	– next to	Parkplatz	– car park
Neffe	– nephew	Parlaments-	– houses of
nehmen	– (to) take	gebäude	parliament
nein	– no	Party	– party
neu	– new	passieren	– (to) happen
nicht	– not	Pferd	– horse
Nichte	– niece	Pflanze	– plant
nichts	– nothing	Pflaume	– plum
nie	– never	Pilot(in)	– pilot
niemand	– nobody	Pink	– pink
nirgendwo	– nowhere	Pinsel	– paintbrush
noch	– still	plötzlich	– suddenly
noch einer	– another	Polizei	– police
nochmals	– again	Pommes frites	– chips (B.E.), fries (A.E.)
normal	– normal		
Nummer	– number	Popgruppe	– pop group
nur	– only	Preis	– price
nur, bloß	– just	Problem	– problem
		Projekt	– project
ob	– if	Pullover	– pullover
oben	– upstairs	Punkt	– full stop
Oberfläche	– surface	putzen	– (to) clean
oder	– or		
öffnen	– (to) open	**R**adiergummi	– rubber
Öffnungszeiten	– opening times	Radio	– radio

Räuber	– robber
rechts	– right
reden	– (to) speak
Regal	– shelf (shelves)
Regen	– rain
Regenschirm	– umbrella
Regenwald	– rainforest
regnen	– (to) rain
reich	– rich
reisen	– (to) travel
Reisende(r)	– passenger
reiten	– horse riding
Restaurant	– restaurant
richtig	– right
riesig	– huge
Robbe	– seal
Rock	– skirt
rot	– red
Rücken, zurück, Rückseite	– back
Saal	– hall
Sache	– object
sagen	– (to) say
Salat	– salad
sammeln	– (to) collect
Sankt	– saint
Satz	– sentence
Säule	– column
Schaf	– sheep
Schal	– scarf
Schere	– (a pair of) scissors
schicken	– (to) send
schieben	– (to) push
Schild	– sign
schlafen	– (to) sleep
Schlafzimmer	– bedroom
schlagen (Ball)	– (to) hit (the ball)
schlecht	– bad
schließen	– (to) close
Schlussverkauf	– sale
Schmuck	– jewellery (B.E.), jewelry (A.E.)
Schmutz	– dirt
schneiden	– (to) cut
schneien	– (to) snow
schnell	– fast, quickly
schön	– nice
Schornstein	– chimney
Schotte	– Scotsman
Schottenrock	– kilt
Schottland	– Scotland
Schrank	– cupboard
schrecklich	– terrible, horrible
schreiben	– (to) write
Schreibtisch	– desk
schreien	– (to) shout
Schuh	– shoe
Schule	– school
Schüler(in)	– pupil
Schulsportplatz	– school field
Schultasche	– schoolbag
Schuluniform	– school uniform
Schuppen	– shed
Schüssel	– bowl
schwarz	– black
(Schwarzes) Brett	– notice board
Schwein	– pig
schwer	– heavy
schwer, schwierig	– difficult
Schwert	– sword
Schwester	– sister
Schwimmbecken	– swimming pool
schwimmen	– (to) swim

See	– lake
segeln	– (to) sail
sehen	– (to) see
sehen, schauen	– (to) look
Sehenswürdigkeiten	– sights
sehr	– very
sein	– his
seltsam	– strange
Sendung	– programme
Sessel	– armchair
setzen, stellen, legen	– (to) put
sich erinnern	– (to) remember
sicher	– safe
sie, ihr	– her
singen	– (to) sing
sitzen	– (to) sit
Sitzreihe	– row
Skateboard	– skateboard
Skelett	– skeleton
Ski fahren	– (to) ski
Skorpion	– scorpion
so	– so
Socken	– (a pair of) socks
Sofa	– sofa
Sohn	– son
sollen	– should
Sommer	– summer
Sonne	– sun
sonnig	– sunny
sorgfältig	– carefully
Spaß	– fun
spät	– (to be) late
Spaziergang	– walk
Speisewagen	– buffet car
Spiel	– game
spielen	– (to) play
Spielplatz	– playground
Sportschuhe	– training shoes, trainers
Sprache	– language
sprechen	– (to) talk, (to) speak
springen	– (to) jump
Stadt	– town
Stadtzentrum	– town centre
stehen	– (to) stand
Stein	– stone
Stimme	– voice
Strand	– beach
Straße	– road, street
Studio	– studio
Stuhl	– chair
Stunde	– an hour
suchen nach	– (to) look for
südlich, Süden	– south, South
super	– super
Supermarkt	– supermarket
Suppe	– soup
surfen	– surfing
süß	– sweet
Sweatshirt	– sweatshirt
Tafel	– (black)board
Tag	– day
täglich	– daily, every day
Tante	– aunt
tanzen	– (to) dance
Tasche	– bag
Tasse	– cup
Teddybär	– teddy bear
Tee	– tea
Teenager	– teenager
Teich	– pond
Teil	– part
Teller	– plate
Tennis	– tennis

Teppich	– carpet
teuer	– expensive
Text	– text
Tier	– animal
Tisch	– table
Tochter	– daughter
Toilette	– toilet
toll, fantastisch	– great
toll!, super!	– wow!
Tomate	– tomato
Tor	– gate
Tour	– tour
Tourist(in)	– tourist
tragen	– (to) carry, (to) wear
traurig	– sad
treffen	– (to) meet
Treppe	– stairs
Treppenabsatz	– landing
trinken	– (to) drink
Tschüs	– bye
T-Shirt	– T-shirt
Tür	– door
Türklingel	– doorbell
Turm	– tower
Türschwelle	– doorstep
typisch	– typical
U-Bahn	– underground
über	– across, over
überall	– everywhere
überhaupt nicht	– not (…) at all
übernachten	– (to) stay
Überraschung	– surprise
(3) Uhr	– (3) o'clock
um (Uhrzeit)	– at
um (…) herum	– around
und	– and
uneben	– uneven
ungefähr	– about
unglücklich	– unhappy
Uniform	– uniform
uns	– us
(nach) unten	– downstairs
unter	– under
Unterricht	– lesson
Unterteller	– saucer
Urlaub	– holiday
Vater	– father
vergessen	– (to) forget
verheiratet	– married
verkaufen	– (to) sell
verlassen	– (to) leave
verlieren	– (to) lose
vermuten	– (to) guess
verpassen	– (to) miss
verschieden	– different
verschwunden	– missing
verstehen	– (to) understand
viel(e)	– (a) lot of, many
vielleicht	– maybe
Viertel (nach/vor)	– (a) quarter (past/to)
Vogel	– bird
von	– by, of
von, aus	– from
vor (*Zeit*)	– before, ago
vor (*Ort*)	– in front of
vorbeigehen	– (to) go past, (to) pass (by)
Vorderseite	– front
Vorsicht	– caution
Wagen	– cart
wahnsinnig	– mad, insane
wahrscheinlich	– probably
Wand	– wall

wann?	– when?
warm	– warm
warten	– (to) wait
warum?	– why?
was?, welche/-r/-s?	– what?
was ist los?	– what's wrong?
was ist mit …?	– what about …?
waschen	– (to) wash
Wasser	– water
Weg	– path
weglaufen	– (to) run away
Wegweiser	– signpost
wehtun	– (to) hurt
weil	– because
weiß	– white
weit (weg)	– far (away)
weiterfahren	– (to) drive on
weitergehen	– (to) go on
welche/-r/-s?	– which?
Welle	– wave
Welpe	– puppy
wenige	– few
wenn, falls	– if
wer?	– who?
werfen	– (to) throw
wessen?	– whose?
Wetter	– weather
Wetterbericht	– weather report
wie	– how, like
wie alt?	– how old?
wie viel?	– how many?
wie viel Uhr?	– what time?
wie viele?	– how many?
Wildpark	– wildlife park
Willkommen	– welcome
windig	– windy
Winter	– winter
wirklich	– really
wissen	– (to) know
Witz	– joke
witzig	– funny
wo?	– where?
Woche	– week
Wochenende	– weekend
Wohltätigkeitslauf	– fun-run
wohnen	– (to) live
Wohnviertel	– residential area
Wohnzimmer	– living room
Wolfshund	– wolfhound
wollen	– (to) want (to)
Wort	– word
Zahl	– number
Zahnschmerzen	– toothache
Zaun	– fence
zeichnen	– (to) draw
zeigen	– (to) show
Zeit	– time
Zeitung	– newspaper
Zeitungen austragen	– (to) deliver newspapers
Zentrum	– centre
Zimmer	– room
zu, nach	– to
zu Hause	– home
zu verkaufen	– (on) sale
Zug	– train
zum Beispiel	– for example
zurück	– (to) return, back
zusammen	– together
zweite/-r/-s	– second
zwischen	– between

Key –
Lösungen zu den Aufgaben

- Damit du sie schneller findest, wurden viele der Lösungen **farbig hervorgehoben.**

- Beachte, dass es oft mehr als nur eine einzige richtige Antwort gibt. Die verschiedenen Möglichkeiten sind durch Schrägstriche voneinander getrennt, in Klammern stehende Wörter oder Satzteile können entfallen.

- Die Lösungen bei Textproduktion oder Sprachmittlung sind oft als Vorschlag zu verstehen. Lass dich deshalb nicht entmutigen, wenn dein Text von der hier angegebenen Musterlösung abweicht.

- Prüfe bitte auch deine Rechtschreibung genau. Wenn deine Lösung falsch war, solltest du die Übung später noch einmal wiederholen. Dazu kannst du Stellen, an denen du Fehler gemacht hast, hier in der Lösung farbig markieren. So findest du sie später schnell wieder.

Reading

Topic 1: Seal Island

1 a) island — ✓ Insel / ☐ Insekt / ☐ Ausland
  b) (to) live — ☐ lieben / ☐ lächeln / ✓ leben
  c) river — ☐ Meer / ✓ Fluss / ☐ See
  d) neighbour — ☐ Nachfolger / ☐ Nachbarland / ✓ Nachbar(in)
  e) bridge — ☐ Unterführung / ✓ Brücke / ☐ Bahnübergang
  f) people — ✓ Leute / ☐ Erwachsene / ☐ Kinder

2

House Number	Who lives there?
1	Tina and her family
2	Robert and his family
3	Harry
4	Karen and her family
5	Jane
6	Peter, Kim
7	Kathy, her three children, Slipper (dog)
8	Mary
9	Freddy

3 Textabschnitte, die markiert werden sollten:
  a) "All the houses […] are nice" (Z. 2/3)
  b) "Kathy, her three children […]" (Z. 3), "Peter and Kim are their neighbours." (Z. 4/5)
  c) "Slipper and the children playing in the river" (Z. 7/8)
  d) vgl. c
  e) "The children go to school on the island." (Z. 9/10)

f) "Jane likes loud music" (Z. 11/12)
g) "Karen, Tina and Robert live in the three houses near the shop with their families." (Z. 14–16)
h) "Karen, Tina [...] live near the shop [...]. Tina's got a boat and Karen's got a big garden." (14–18)

4
		true	false
a)	There are one or two nice houses on the island.		✓

(This is false because) All the houses are nice.

b)	Kim lives near children.	✓	
c)	Slipper likes water.	✓	
d)	Kathy's children have fun in the river.	✓	
e)	There isn't a teacher on the island.		✓

(This is false because) There is a school on the island.

| f) | Jane listens to quiet music. | | ✓ |

(This is false because) Jane listens to loud music.

| g) | Only three people live near the shop. | | ✓ |

(This is false because) Three families live near the shop.

| h) | Karen's neighbour has got a boat. | ✓ | |

5
a) three / Kathy has got three children.
b) Jane / Jane hasn't got a neighbour.
c) no / No, there isn't. (There is a small shop on the island.)
d) yes / Yes, they have.

Topic 2: Cranberry Hall

6 a) Prospekt
 b) Layout (Überschrift, Anordnung des Textes), Foto
 c) Man erhält Informationen zu einer Sehenswürdigkeit (Cranberry Hall): mögliche Aktivitäten, Öffnungszeiten, Preise

7

A	B	C	D	E
4	3	1	5	2

8

		true	false
a)	Cranberry Hall is 249 years old.		✓
b)	Cranberry Hall is open on Tuesdays.	✓	
c)	The adventure playground is new.		✓
d)	The museum is open for 9 hours every day.	✓	
e)	The animals are in the gardens.		✓
f)	The gardens are not open on Sundays.		✓
g)	Cranberry Hall is nice for families.	✓	
h)	You don't pay to go into the park.	✓	

9 a) Yes, you can.
 b) Yes, it is.
 c) The museum is open first.
 d) Yes, it is.
 e) No, there isn't.

10

A	B	C	D	E	F
5	6	1	2	3	4

11

Places in Cranberry Hall	museum, adventure playground, big gardens, park
Opening hours (Öffnungszeiten)	Cranberry Hall and adventure playground: Monday, Tuesday, Friday, Saturday 10 a.m.–5 p.m. museum: every day 9 a.m.–6 p.m. park and gardens: every day
Price	adults: £ 9.25; children: £ 4.25
Things to see in the museum	old cars
Things to do in the park	walk, ride a bike, play games (watch animals)

12

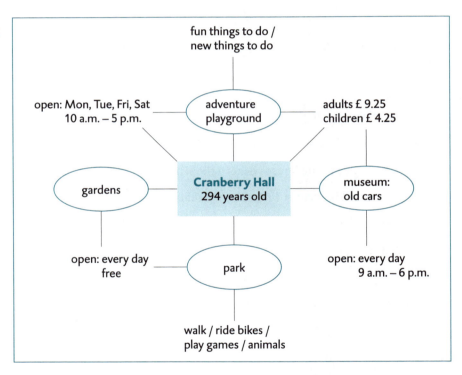

Topic 3: The village school

13

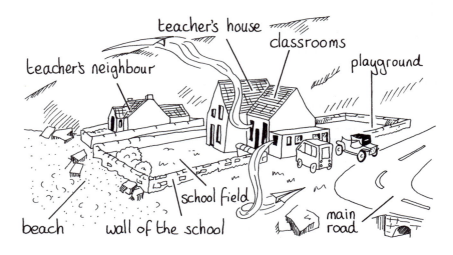

14
a) The school isn't in England. — **true** ✓
b) There are a lot of classrooms in the school. — **false** ✓
c) The teachers live in the houses next to the school. — **false** ✓
d) The playground is small but the school field isn't. — **false** ✓
e) The beach is behind the school. — **false** ✓
f) The road goes to the village. — **true** ✓
g) There is a big village one mile away. — **false** ✓
h) Some children can get a bus to school. — **true** ✓

15
a) You are in the school bus next to the car.
Which is the first building, then the second and then the last?
☐ teacher's house, classrooms, neighbour's house
✓ classrooms, teacher's house, neighbour's house
☐ neighbour's house, teacher's house, classrooms

Topic 3: The village school

This is a photo of a small school in Scotland. The school is on the Isle of Skye. There are only two classrooms in the school. One teacher lives in the house next to the classrooms. The teacher's neighbour lives in the house behind the school. The other teacher lives in the town 15 miles away.

The school has got a school field and a playground. They are not very big because there aren't a lot of children here. The playground is in front of the car on the right. The school field has got a wall and the beach is in front of it.

The road next to the school is the main road to the village. The village is very small – it has only got twenty houses. The village is about one mile away and the village children walk to school. The other children come by a small bus.

Vocabulary

(to) live in: *wohnen in*
school field: *Sportplatz der Schule*
main road: *Hauptstraße*
behind: *hinter*
playground: *(hier) Schulhof*
beach: *(hier) Küste*

b) You are looking out of the classroom window.
   What is the first thing you see, then the second and then the last?
   ☐ playground, school field, wall
   ☐ school field, beach, wall
   ☑ school field, wall, beach

c) Whose car is in the picture – probably?
   ☐ the neighbour's car
   ☑ the teacher's car from the town
   ☐ a pupil's car

d) It is winter and there is a lot of snow. Who is at school first?
   ☑ the teacher in the house, because _he / she lives next to the school._
   ☐ the teacher from the town, because _____
   ☐ the children from the village, because _____

Topic 4: The ghost train

16

1	2	3	4	5	6	7	8	9
C	G	E	B	A	D	I	H	F

C KIRSTY: Cool! That's scary.
G POLLY: What's scary, Kirsty?
E KIRSTY: The ghost train. 5 C have got a ghost train in their classroom. It's for the school party.
B POLLY: Oh no, not again. Mr Black and 5 C always have a ghost train. The first time you see it, it's very good but then after that it's always the same.
A KIRSTY: It's different this year, Polly. It's great. There's a ghost of an old woman. She stands next to you, then she tells you a terrible story – a story about a big fire in the school in 1847. At the end of the story a skeleton pushes you away. Then there's the man without a head and some other things, but the old woman, she's so real – it's very scary, Polly.
D *(Polly goes on the ghost train)*
I POLLY: It's boring. Last year – this year – next year – it's always the same; a skeleton, the man without a head and some other things.

H KIRSTY: But ... the old woman, Polly? Isn't she great?
F POLLY: Kirsty, there isn't an old woman – every year it's the same!

17 a) **ghost train** ☑ Geisterbahn   b) **scary** ☐ süß
        ☐ U-Bahn   ☐ aufregend
        ☐ Fahrbahn   ☑ furchterregend

   c) **(the) same** ☐ anderes   d) **skeleton** ☐ Knochen
        ☐ Gegenteil   ☑ Skelett
        ☑ derselbe (die-/das-)   ☐ Körper

   e) **without** ☑ ohne   f) **real** ☑ echt/real
        ☐ mit   ☐ wirklich
        ☐ aus   ☐ falsch

18 a) Who has got the ghost train? **5 C** have got the ghost train.
   b) Where is the ghost train? The ghost train is in their **classroom.**
   c) Who is 5 C's teacher? **Mr Black** is 5 C's teacher.
   d) What is the old woman? The old woman is a **ghost.**
   e) What pushes you away? A **skeleton** pushes you away.
   f) What hasn't the man got? The man hasn't got a **head.**

19

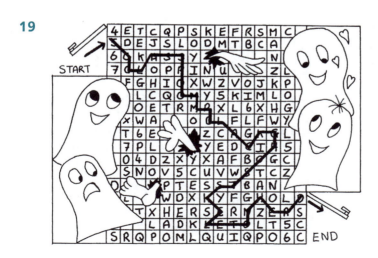

20 a) Kirsty is talking to Polly.
b) They've got / 5C have got a ghost train in their classroom for the school party.
c) It is always the same.
d) The old woman's story is about a big fire in the school in 1847.
e) The old woman isn't there.

Topic 5: Hi Dave, …

21

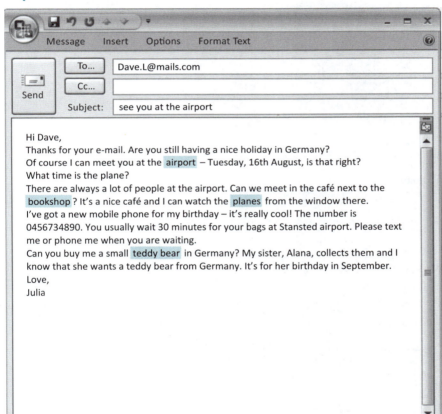

22 Vergleiche Markierungen im Text bei Aufgabe 21.

23 a) Dave is ...
- [ ] working in Germany.
- [✓] having a holiday in Germany.
- [ ] living in Germany.

b) Dave asks Julia to meet him on ...
- [ ] Monday.
- [✓] Tuesday.
- [ ] Wednesday.

c) Where can Dave find Julia?

A [ ]   B [ ]   C [✓]

d) Dave waits for ... for his bags.
- [ ] a quarter of an hour
- [✓] half an hour
- [ ] one hour

e) Does Julia like her present?
- [✓] Yes, she does.
- [ ] No, she doesn't.
- [ ] She hasn't got a present.

f) Does Julia's sister have a lot of teddy bears?
   - [✓] Yes, she does.
   - [ ] No, she doesn't.
   - [ ] The answer isn't in the e-mail.

24
a) Dave is in Germany.
b) No, she doesn't. (She meets Dave.)
c) Yes, she can.
d) Alana's present is small.
e) No, they aren't. (Alana's is in September but Julia's isn't.)

25 I'm **waiting** for my two **bags**. Are you in the **café**? I've got the **teddy bear** for your **sister**. Oh, here come my **bags** now! Dave

Topic 6: The Scotsman

26

A	B	C	D	E	F
3	5	4	1	6	2

27 (Musterlösung)
a) What does Duffy pick up?
b) How big is the man?
c) Where is the bread?
d) Why does the Scotsman run away?
e) Who says 'Good morning'?

28 a) Where is Duffy's camera?

A [✓]

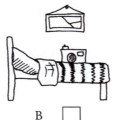
B [ ]

C [ ]

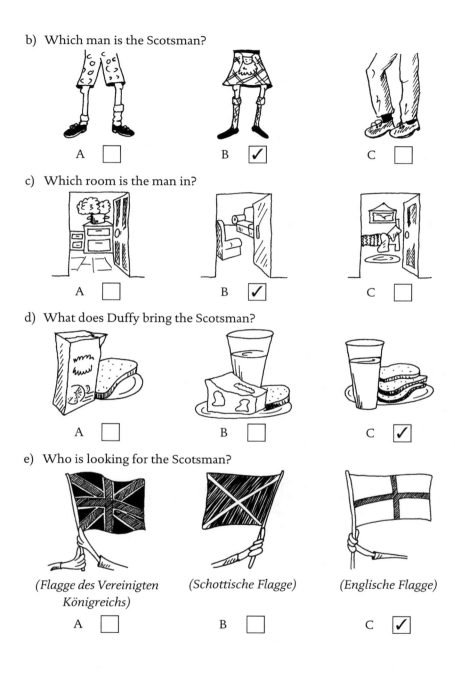

f) Who is Mrs Macdonald?

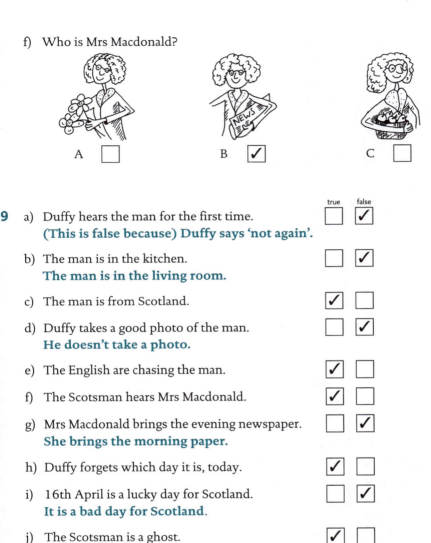

A ☐   B ✓   C ☐

	true	false
29 a) Duffy hears the man for the first time. **(This is false because) Duffy says 'not again'.**	☐	✓
b) The man is in the kitchen. **The man is in the living room.**	☐	✓
c) The man is from Scotland.	✓	☐
d) Duffy takes a good photo of the man. **He doesn't take a photo.**	☐	✓
e) The English are chasing the man.	✓	☐
f) The Scotsman hears Mrs Macdonald.	✓	☐
g) Mrs Macdonald brings the evening newspaper. **She brings the morning paper.**	☐	✓
h) Duffy forgets which day it is, today.	✓	☐
i) 16th April is a lucky day for Scotland. **It is a bad day for Scotland.**	☐	✓
j) The Scotsman is a ghost.	✓	☐

30 a) The noises come from downstairs / the living-room.
 b) The Scotsman is two metres (tall) and he wears / is wearing a kilt.
 c) The man wants bread and water / … something to eat and drink.
 d) The Scotsman runs away because he thinks the English are coming.

31 Was geschah bevor der Text beginnt? Wähle die beste Beschreibung aus.
- [ ] A man takes photos of a ghost.
- [ ] There is a battle *(Schlacht)*.
- [x] A man often hears noises in his house.

Topic 7: I hate shopping!

32 a) **(to) have to**
- [ ] hassen
- [x] müssen
- [ ] brauchen

b) **(to) grow into**
- [x] in etwas hineinwachsen
- [ ] hineinbringen
- [ ] größer werden

c) **(to) go cycling**
- [ ] Ski fahren
- [ ] fahren
- [x] Fahrrad fahren

d) **sale**
- [x] Schlussverkauf
- [ ] segeln
- [ ] kaufen

e) **better**
- [ ] gut
- [x] besser
- [ ] schlechter

f) **enough**
- [ ] viele
- [ ] wenige
- [x] genug

33

A	B	C	D	E	F
5	6	4	1	2	3

Sam doesn't like shopping with his mum.
Sam needs some new school clothes.
Sam's mother doesn't buy expensive training shoes for school.
Sam wants what his friends have got.
They are going to one shop because it has got a sale.
Sam thinks the shop in George Street is good.

34

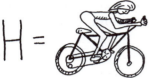  

Topic 8: Dick Whittington

35

A	B	C	D	E	F	G	H
3	7	8	5	1	2	6	4

		true	false
36	a) Dick doesn't like where he lives.	✓	
	b) Dick goes to London in the afternoon. **Dick goes to London in the morning.**		✓
	c) A man takes him to London.	✓	
	d) Dick is happy in London. **Dick isn't happy in London because he is cold, hungry, poor and he's got nowhere to sleep.**		✓
	e) Dick has no friends so he buys a cat. **Dick buys a cat because there are mice in his room.**		✓
	f) Mr Fitzwarren buys clothes from the Sultan. **The Sultan buys clothes from Mr Fitzwarren.**		✓
	g) There are usually mice on the boat.	✓	
	h) The cat stays with Dick. **Mr Fitzwarren takes the cat with him.**		✓

i) There are no cats in Barbary. ✓ ☐

j) The money comes from Mr Fitzwarren. ☐ ✓
   The money comes from the Sultan.

37 In London, Dick has got **nowhere** to sleep. Mrs Fitzwarren gives him **work** and somewhere to **sleep**. But there are mice in his **bedroom**. Dick **buys** a cat and the cat **eats** the mice. Then, Mr Fitzwarren tells Dick about the **mice** on his boat. Dick gives Mr Fitzwarren his **cat** and very soon there are no mice on the **boat**. In Barbary, the Sultan is very **sad / unhappy** because there are mice everywhere there, too. Mr Fitzwarren gives the Sultan **Dick's** cat. Dick's cat then eats all the mice in **Barbary** and the Sultan is **happy** again. The Sultan sends Dick a **present** to say thank you. The Sultan's present makes Dick a **rich** man.

Topic 9: Four days in America

38

A	B	C	D	E
5	6	4	1	3

39

Topic 10: Sebastian's problem

40

Story part	Heading
5	Jenny saves the day
4	Sebastian's story
3	Miss Roberts is angry
6	One problem after the other
2	The boring story
1	The new teacher

41

1	2	3	4	5	6
D	F	A	B	E	C

Listening

Topic 11: No names!

Listening text 1

TEACHER: So, Chloe. Here are the pictures.
CHLOE: Jenny's picture has got people in it.
TEACHER: But, Chloe, there are two pictures with people in them. Let's start with the car. Whose picture is that?
CHLOE: It's not a girl's picture – girls don't draw cars.
TEACHER: That's a big help, Chloe. And what's this?
CHLOE: It's a picture of water.
TEACHER: Water?
CHLOE: Yes, that picture is mine.
TEACHER: Good, that's one picture with a name. And … the picture of the fish?
CHLOE: That's my friend's picture.
TEACHER: Chloe! Are you helping me or not? Who's your friend?
CHLOE: Mike's sister.
TEACHER: Chloe! You're not helping me very much.
CHLOE: Look! There's Robert's picture – the people in the park.
TEACHER: Thank you, Chloe. Now I can give all the pictures back.

Listening text 2

Track 2

I want to put all your pictures on the wall. We need three pictures for the top. Mike, can you put your picture of the car in the middle. Super.

Jenny, put the two pictures with people next to the car. That's your picture, the people in a disco, and Robert's picture, the people in the park. The disco can go on the left.

Now, … water and fish go together. Chloe, put the fish under Robert and Mike's pictures … and next to it, the picture of the water.

Now, let me look at them. Yes, … they look good on that wall. What do you think?

42

	fish	car	people in a disco	people in a park	water
Chloe	✗	✗	✗	✗	✓
Laura	✓	✗	✗	✗	✗
Jenny	✗	✗	✓	✗	✗
Robert	✗	✗	✗	✓	✗
Mike	✗	✓	✗	✗	✗

43 There are no **names** on the pictures. Chloe is helping her **teacher**. Chloe's help **isn't** very good. Chloe says Mike's **sister** painted a **fish**. She is Chloe's **friend**. Chloe then **tells** the teacher who painted the people in the **park**. The teacher can now **give** the pictures back to the children.

44

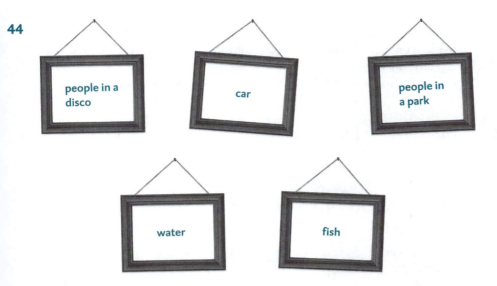

Topic 12: Let's play football – for girls, too

Track 3

Listening text
WENDY: Hi, Max!
MAX: Hi, Wendy.
WENDY: Where's Tony? – Doing his homework?
MAX: Doing his homework! That's a joke! There's his school bag. He's playing a computer game in Mrs Green's classroom. Jake and Dave are with him, too.
WENDY: What! That's not fair. They're never here when there is something to do. What about the school party? The boys have to help, too!
MAX: I'm here!
WENDY: Yes, I know, but the other boys aren't. I'm not waiting for them! I've got an idea. Come on, girls! Jenny, bring that bag from over there – let's play football.
MAX: Wendy, wait.
WENDY: No. They can wait for us or there's no party!
(Wendy und die Mädchen verlassen das Klassenzimmer. Einige Minuten später kommen Tony und seine Freunde herein.)
TONY: Hi, Max.
MAX: Hi, Tony.
TONY: Where are the girls? We've got work to do for the party.
MAX: They're not here. They've …

TONY: Typical! They're always late. The boys always have to do the girls' work ... but not this time! I'm not waiting for them, Max. Let's play football.
MAX: Tony, the girls ...
TONY: Get the ball, Max. It's in my bag over there. – Hey, where's my bag?

45 a) joke   A <u>joke</u> is a funny story.   **Witz**
    b) not fair   It's <u>not fair</u> when you do all the work.   **unfair**
    c) something   Can we do <u>something</u> for the party?   **etwas**
    d) have to   You <u>have to</u> go to school.   **müssen**
    e) typical   That's <u>typical</u>! They're always late.   **typisch**

46 a) Where is Tony?

b) What must the pupils do?

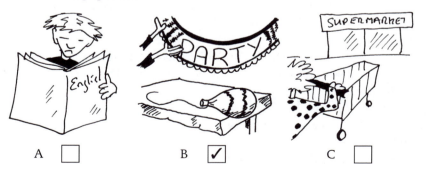

c) Who takes the bag?

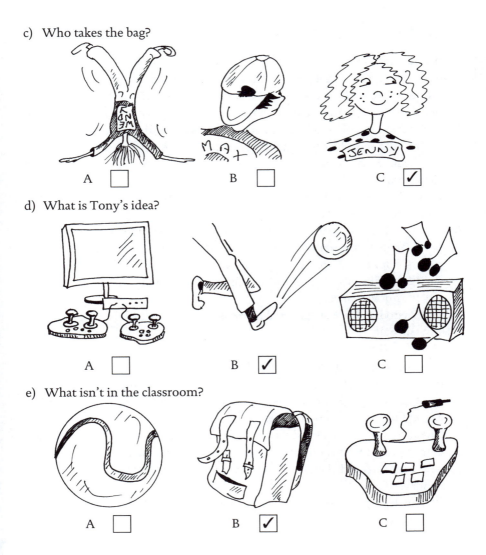

d) What is Tony's idea?

e) What isn't in the classroom?

7 The boys and **girls** have to make their classroom **nice** for a **party**. Max is in the **classroom** and then Wendy **arrives / comes**. She asks where the other **boys** are. She is angry because the boys are **playing** computer games. She and her **friend**, Jenny, take Tony's **bag / ball**. When Tony arrives, he is angry **because** the girls aren't there. He thinks the boys always have to do all the **work**. He tells Max to get his ball, then they can play **football**. His ball is in the bag. But his **bag** isn't there.

Topic 13: Work and school

Listening text

Track 4

JOHN: Hi, I'm John. I'm 15 years old and I live in the South of England. At school we're making a short radio programme about pupils and work. So here I am – it's quarter past six in the morning, I'm just walking along Front Street and I'm going to Mrs Green's house next – and it's wet and cold. But Sally's with me. She's holding the microphone and she's wet and cold, too. Say hello, Sally, so we know you're here and not sitting in a nice warm classroom.

SALLY: Hi! I'm here – and it really is quarter past six and I'm wet and really cold, too. So John, start talking or I'm going home.

JOHN: Okay. I always wake up at half past five because I deliver the morning newspapers to people's houses. I have a wash and then I collect the newspapers from the shop. I usually start work at six. I have about 100 newspapers to deliver – it's nice in the summer but in winter or when it's raining, it's not very nice.

SALLY: Like today! It's wet, cold and horrible ...

JOHN: Sssh, Sally ...

SALLY: Sorry. Go on.

JOHN: I stop work at quarter to eight. Then I go home for my breakfast and get ready for school. I walk to school and arrive there at about ten to nine. I go to King George's Comprehensive School. It's a normal school and the last lesson finishes at half past three.

After school I go home and do my homework. Then I have dinner with my family, watch television, play a computer game or see my friends. I go to bed about 9 o'clock, because I work every morning – but not on Saturday or Sunday.

SALLY: Can I go now? It's really cold and horrible ... How can you do this, John?

48

Englisch	Bild	Deutsch	Englisch	Bild	Deutsch
programme	F	Sendung	(to) deliver	B	austragen
(to) hold	D	festhalten	newspapers	C	Zeitungen
(to) wake up	E	aufwachen	(to) get ready	A	sich fertig machen

49 a)

b) At 5.30 a.m. John wakes up.
At 6.00 a.m. John starts work.
At 7.45 a.m. John stops / finishes work.
At 8.50 a.m. John is / arrives at school.
At 3.30 p.m. John finishes school / school ends.
At 9.00 p.m. John goes to sleep.

50 a) **15 / fifteen** b) **no** c) **John**
d) **no** e) **no** f) **no**

g) **washes** h) **summer** i) **walks**
j) **George** k) **no** l) **yes**
m) **no**

51

- clock: It's not ten to nine, it's quarter past six.
- street sign: They are not in Green Street, they are in Front Street.
- camera: Sally isn't holding a camera, she's holding a microphone.
- books: John isn't delivering books, he's delivering newspapers.
- shorts: John isn't wearing shorts, because it's wet and cold.
- face: John is 15 and the person here has got a beard.
- "kidz" könnte ebenfalls als Fehler angesehen werden, weil man eigentlich "kids" schreiben müsste. Die Schreibung "kidz" ist allerdings typisch für Graffiti.

Topic 14: A short story about eyes

Track 5

Listening text

It's November and it's late in the evening. Steve and Jane are walking home after a friend's party. They are the only two people in the street and it's dark. Steve suddenly sees two eyes watching them. He says to Jane, "I think somebody is watching us – I can see their eyes."

Jane is frightened. "Where are the eyes, Steve? Are they still watching us?" she asks in a quiet voice.

Steve tells her the eyes are in the big tree. She looks and sees them. "Who is it?" she asks.

"I don't know but can you run, Jane?" Steve says.

Jane answers, "Yes." Steve tells her to run after three. "One, two, three – run!" says Steve, and they run and run until they are home. Jane opens the door and closes it quickly – safe from those terrible eyes.

"People are funny," the cat thinks, as it closes its eyes and goes to sleep.

52 a) It is **dark** at 11.30 in the evening.   **dunkel**
b) Can **somebody** help me, please?   **jemand**
c) I am **frightened** of snakes.   **Angst haben**
d) He reads **until** 7 o'clock.   **bis**
e) She can run **quickly**.   **schnell**
f) Your money is **safe** in a bank.   **sicher**

53 (*mögliche* key words)

Key words
November,
late, evening   Steve and Jane walking home
the only people in the street
two eyes watching
frightened   eyes in tree
run home
cat closes its eyes

(*Musterlösung*)
Es ist November, und es ist spät und dunkel. Zwei Leute, Jane und Steve, sind auf dem Weg nach Hause. Außer ihnen ist niemand auf der Straße, aber Jane und Steve sehen, dass sie zwei Augen von einem Baum aus beobachten. Sie haben Angst und beschließen, so schnell wie möglich nach Hause zu laufen. Was sie gesehen haben, war jedoch nur eine Katze.

54
a) The party is in summer. ☐ ✓
   The party is in November / in autumn.
b) There are two more people in the street. ☐ ✓
   There are only two people in the street: Steve and Jane
c) Steve sees the eyes first. ✓ ☐
d) Jane doesn't like the eyes. ✓ ☐
e) Jane sees the eyes in the house. ☐ ✓
   Jane sees the eyes in the tree.
f) The people run home. ✓ ☐
g) Steve closes the door. ☐ ✓
   Jane closes the door.
h) There is a cat in the tree. ✓ ☐

55

It's _very_ _dark_ tonight.
I think I can _see_ _eyes_.
Somebody _is_ _watching_ us.
In _the_ _trees_, _over_ _there_.
Where?
Let's _run_!

Topic 15: Singleton Hall

Listening text

Singleton Hall is a big old house in England. Today is Monday, and Carol is in the garden. Near the tree she sees a ball. She walks towards it and then she sees two children. "What are you two doing at Singleton Hall?" she asks.

"We're playing with our ball. And who are you?" the girl asks Carol. "Why are you at Singleton Hall?"

Carol looks at the boy and the girl and then says, "I live here. Who are you?"

"I'm Robert and this is Mary, and we live here, too," says the boy.

"No you don't," says Carol. But the children aren't listening and they run away.

Carol then walks to the house. Her brother, Chris, is sitting on a chair looking at some old photographs. Carol tells him the story about the children. "That's strange, Carol, I always see them on Mondays, too," he says. "Come here and look at these photos. This is in March, 1912. You can see the Singleton family with their children. There's a boy and a girl. Now, read the back of the photo."

Carol reads the back of the photo. It says, 'Mr and Mrs Singleton and their two children, Robert and Mary, at Singleton Hall, March 1912'.

"I think we've got two ghosts," says Chris.

a) I walk **towards** the tree.
   ☐ nach ☑ in Richtung ☐ über

b) We **live** in a big old house.
   ☐ schlafen ☐ arbeiten ☑ wohnen

c) The children **run away** from the woman.
   ☑ weglaufen ☐ gehen ☐ kommen

d) It is a **strange** story about the children.
   ☐ lustig ☑ merkwürdig ☐ fröhlich

e) Mary's photo is here. Her name is on the **back** of it.
   ☐ Vorderseite ☑ Rückseite ☐ Seite

f) The old house has got a **ghost**.
   ☐ Clown ☐ Hund ☑ Gespenst

57 a) Which house is Singleton Hall?

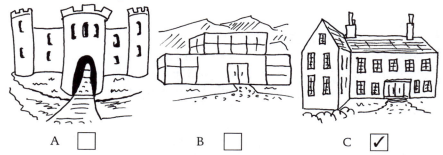

A ☐ B ☐ C ✓

b) Where is the ball?

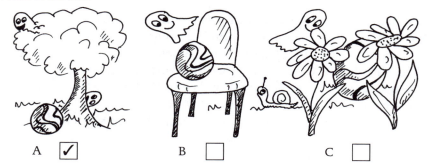

A ✓ B ☐ C ☐

c) How many children are there? – **two**

d) Who talks to Carol first? – **the girl**

e) What is Chris doing?

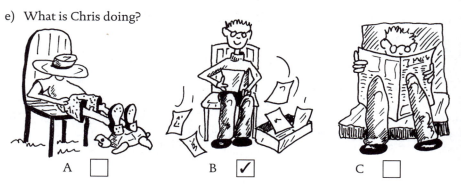

A ☐ B ✓ C ☐

f) When does Chris see the children? – **on Mondays**

g) Which photo are they looking at?

A ✓ B ☐ C ☐

h) What are the children? – **ghosts**

58 Carol lives in an **old** house. Today she is in the **garden**. She sees two **children** and talks to them. Then they **run away** from Carol. Carol then **talks to / asks** her brother about the children in the garden. Her brother is **looking** at some old **photographs / photos**. Chris shows them to Carol. He asks her to read the **back** of one photograph. Chris thinks the children are **ghosts**.

59

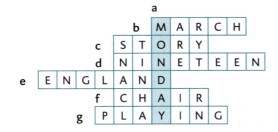

Topic 16: The fun-run

Listening text

TEACHER: Every year at Park School we have a fun-run. We collect money for a village in Africa. The teachers and the pupils run around the school for money.
Because you are all new here I want to tell you about the village in Africa. I've got some photos but first listen to a message from one of the children there.

Key – Listening

KARANI: Hello. My name is Karani. I'm thirteen years old. I've got three brothers and two sisters. I go to school in Sendera in Kenya. At school I read and write in English and I like Music and Maths. My school has got one classroom, forty-two children and a teacher.
My parents have got a small farm. My family is poor. My house has only got one room. My village hasn't got a shop, a bus, or a train and we must walk five kilometres to a doctor and two kilometres to collect water. My brothers, sisters and I collect the water before school starts and after school we help our parents on the farm.

TEACHER: And that's why we collect money for this village. So that we can help them. The fun-run is in two weeks. Here's a letter to your parents about it. Now for the photos.

60
fun-run	*Spaziergang*	*Langlauf*	*Wohltätigkeitslauf*
around	*über*	*unter*	*um … herum*
message	*Massage*	*Nachricht*	*Nachrichten*
years old	*Alter*	*Jubiläum*	*Jahre alt*
farm	*Bahnhof*	*Bauernhof*	*Tiergarten*
doctor	*Arzt, Ärztin*	*Mechaniker(in)*	*Maler(in)*

61
a) There is a **fun-run** at school to get money for poor people.
b) My leg hurts. I must go to the **doctor**.
c) I am 12 **years old**.
d) There are lots of animals on the **farm**.
e) There is a **message** for you from Tina.
f) We must run **around** the school.

62
a) • **teachers**
   • **pupils**
b) **13**
c) **5**
d) • **Music**
   • **Maths**
e) **1**
f) **42**
g) **no**
h) **no**
i) **1**
j) **no**
k) **no**

Key – Listening / 213

63

		true	false
a)	Park School is in Africa.		✓
b)	The fun-run is at school.	✓	
c)	The teacher reads Karani's e-mail.		✓
d)	Karani's class is big.	✓	
e)	Karani can walk to a doctor.	✓	
f)	The water is not in Karani's village.	✓	
g)	Karani works after school.	✓	
h)	The money goes to Karani's family.		✓
i)	The teacher hasn't got the photos with him today.		✓

64

Foto	Passt zu Karani	Beschreibung
A	✓	her school
B	✓	her family's farm
C	–	–
D	–	–
E	✓	Her family are collecting water. / collecting water
F	–	–

Topic 17: Attention, please!

Listening text 1
This is a message for all passengers for the 16.10 train to Manchester. This train is now about 35 minutes late. We are very sorry about this. Because this train is late, the 16.44 train from Newcastle now arrives at platform 5 and not platform 7. Please, can all passengers for Newcastle go to platform 5. Old people or people with heavy bags can get help from our staff on platform 7.

Listening text 2
Here is some information for all our passengers today. The new restaurant on platform 8 is now open. You can buy hot or cold meals there from 8 o'clock in

the morning to 9 o'clock at night. It also has sandwiches, cakes and drinks. Because some EastRail trains are late today, passengers for those trains can get a free hot drink in the restaurant but you must have your ticket with you. Please remember to take all your bags with you, too.

65
a) The people on a train are the **passengers**.   **Fahrgäste**
b) A train stops at a **platform** in a station.   **Gleis / Bahnsteig**
c) 50 kilos is a **heavy** bag.   **schwer**
d) Forty people work at the station.
   These people are the **staff**.   **Mitarbeiter**
e) The drink is **free**. It costs nothing.   **kostenlos**
f) You must buy a **ticket** to go on the train.   **Fahrkarte**

66
a) am Bahnhof (in der Bahnhofshalle oder am Bahnsteig) oder im Zug
b) *(mögliche Stichpunkte)*
   - Jemand will mit dem Zug fahren und es gibt Verspätungen.
   - Für den Zug nach Newcastle gibt es eine Gleisänderung.
   - Es gibt Hilfsangebote für bestimmte Personen.

67
a) What time is the train to Manchester today?

A ☐   B ☐   C ✓

b) Which train isn't late?

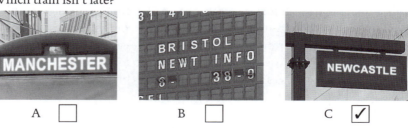

A ☐   B ☐   C ✓

c) Which is the platform for the train to Newcastle today?

A ☐   B ✓   C ☐

d) Who can get help?

A ✓   B ☐   C ☐

68

A	B	C	D	E	F	G	H
✓	–	✓	✓	–	✓	✓	–

Topic 18: Crime Stop

Listening text

PRESENTER: Good evening and welcome to Crime Stop. Tonight, we've got six new stories for you. But first the Bristol police are looking for two bank robbers. Can you help? Inspector Roberts …

POLICEMAN: Good evening, my name is Inspector Roberts from the Bristol police. We're looking for two bank robbers and maybe you know them.
The man is 1 metre 79 and about 30 years old. He has got glasses and black hair. He's wearing a blue shirt, white trousers with black shoes, and he has got a baseball cap, too. The other bank robber is 1 metre 62 tall and about 24 years old. She has got short blonde hair and she's wearing a big T-shirt with the number 11 on it, a pair of jeans and white trainers.
They've got a small red car. The number is AWK 59 EB. We need your help. If you know these people, then phone us – the Bristol police. Our phone number is 0961/3629.

69

Englisch	bank robber	baseball cap	glasses	trainers
Bild	B	C	D	A
Deutsch	Bankräuber	Baseballkappe	Brille	Sportschuhe

70
- The **bank robber** is in the bank.
- Kim has got new **trainers** for school.
- Peter is wearing **glasses**. Now he can see!
- Linda has got a **baseball cap** on her head.

71
a) Crime Stop is looking for two bank robbers. — true ✓

b) The man is 1.97 metres. — false ✓
The man is 1.79 metres.

c) He is about 30 years old. — true ✓

d) He has got blonde hair. — false ✓
He has got black hair.

e) He is wearing a blue shirt and black trousers. — false ✓
He is wearing a blue shirt and white trousers.

f) He has got a cap. — true ✓

g) The second bank robber is 42 years old. — false ✓
The second robber is 24 years old.

h) The second bank robber is a man. — false ✓
The second bank robber is a woman.

i) There is a number on the T-shirt. — true ✓

j) The number of the car is AWK 59 EB. — true ✓

k) The telephone number is: 0961/3269. — false ✓
The number is: 0961/3629.

72
- The first bank robber is: **b**
- The second bank robber is: **g**

Topic 19: Radio Boston

Listening text

Track 11

It's 7.15, I'm Lucy Travis and this is Radio Boston.

Well, it's still raining this morning … a nice wet day for everyone again. And there are a lot of problems on the roads, too – so find your umbrella and leave early for work.

Harry has got a lot more stories for me this morning. Hi, Harry! He's laughing at me behind the window in the studio. Harry, give me the stories to read! Where are all the nice stories for me, today, Harry? *(laughs)* That's better!

The band Red Fingers is playing in the North End this evening – their music is great. It's $7.50 at the door of George Stadium, Hill Road, or online it's $6.75 – that's on www.georgestadium.com.

There's a lot happening in Boston Common Park today – live music, dancing … a super day. That starts at 2.30. Let's hope the rain stops for that.

There's a sale today at MusicMan in West Street near Quincy Market. All their CDs and DVDs are half price. Half price! Why am I working, today?

Now it's time for some more music.

73

Bild	A	B	C	D	E
Englisch	studio	half price	rain	sale	umbrella
Deutsch	Studio	halber Preis	Regen	Schlussverkauf	Regenschirm

74

		true	false
a)	It is 6.30 a.m.		✓
b)	It's a nice morning.		✓
c)	Lucy writes the stories.		✓
d)	Harry and Lucy are having some fun today.	✓	
e)	Lucy isn't a Red Finger's fan.		✓
f)	The internet price is $6.75.	✓	
g)	Things are happening in Boston Common Park this afternoon.	✓	
h)	The MusicMan is in West Road.		✓

i) You can buy cheap CDs near Quincy Market ✓ ☐
today.

j) The weather report (= Wetterbericht) is next. ☐ ✓

75

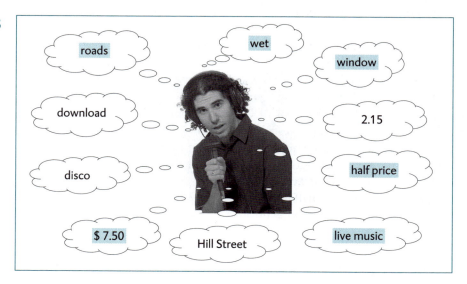

Topic 20: Answering questions

Track 12

Listening text

a) SPEAKER 1: How much is the book?
   SPEAKER 2: ...

b) SPEAKER 1: Can you meet me tonight?
   SPEAKER 2: ...

c) SPEAKER 1: When are we going to Germany?
   SPEAKER 2: ...

d) SPEAKER 1: Excuse me, is this the bus stop for the bus to Oxford?
   SPEAKER 2: ...

e) SPEAKER 1: What is the telephone number for the taxi?
   SPEAKER 2: ...

f) SPEAKER 1: What is your e-mail address?
   SPEAKER 2: ...

g) SPEAKER 1: Where is California?
   SPEAKER 2: ...

Key

a) SPEAKER 1: How much is the book?
   SPEAKER 2: **It's £ 6.99.**

b) SPEAKER 1: Can you meet me tonight?
   SPEAKER 2: **Of course. What time?**

c) SPEAKER 1: When are we going to Germany?
   SPEAKER 2: **In the summer holidays.**

d) SPEAKER 1: Excuse me, is this the bus stop for the bus to Oxford?
   SPEAKER 2: **I'm sorry, I don't know.**

e) SPEAKER 1: What is the telephone number for the taxi?
   SPEAKER 2: **0934 / 20202**

f) SPEAKER 1: What is your e-mail address?
   SPEAKER 2: **It's Tim@aol.com**

g) SPEAKER 1: Where is California?
   SPEAKER 2: **It's in America.**

76 a) ☐ It's 3.15. **What time is it?**
   ☐ It's £ 6.99. **How much is it?**
   ☐ There are six. **How many are they / there?**

b) ☐ After lunch – about 2 o'clock. **What time / When can we meet?**
   ☐ Of course. What time? **Can we meet?**
   ☐ No, I'm sorry. I'm in London tomorrow. **Can we meet tomorrow?**

c) ☐ In the summer holidays. **When are you going to England / France / the USA / ...?**
   ☐ We're watching television. **What are you doing?**
   ☐ Germany is nice. **What is Germany like?**

d) ☐ I like Oxford. **Which town do you like?**
☐ I'm sorry, I don't know. **How far is it?**
☐ No, you must go by train. **Can I walk?**

e) ☐ It's 14 George Street. **What is the address?**
☐ It's about £ 5.00, I think. **How much is it?**
☐ 0934 / 20202 **What is the phone number?**

f) ☐ Two people are waiting. **How many people are waiting?**
☐ There are three bus stops. **How many bus stops are there?**
☐ It's Tim@aol.com **What is your e-mail address?**

g) ☐ My dog's name is Bruce. **What is your dog's name?**
☐ It's in America. **Where is it?**
☐ I'm from Scotland. **Where are you from?**

77 a) ☐ It's 3.15.
✓ It's £ 6.99.
☐ There are six.

b) ☐ After lunch – about 2 o'clock.
✓ Of course. What time?
☐ No, I'm sorry. I'm in London tomorrow.

c) ✓ In the summer holidays.
☐ We're watching television.
☐ Germany is nice.

d) ☐ I like Oxford, too.
✓ I'm sorry, I don't know.
☐ No, you must go by train.

e) ☐ It's 14 George Street.
☐ It's about £ 5.00, I think.
✓ 0934 / 20202

f) ☐ Two people are waiting.
☐ There are three bus stops.
✓ It's Tim@aol.com

g) ☐ My dog's name is Bruce.
✓ It's in America.
☐ I'm from Scotland.

Topic 21: What do you say?

Listening text 1
SPEAKER 1: So, you want a new school bag.
SPEAKER 2: ...
SPEAKER 1: How big do you want it?
SPEAKER 2: ...
SPEAKER 1: And, what colour?
SPEAKER 2: ...
SPEAKER 1: What about this bag? Do you like it?
SPEAKER 2: ...

Key
SPEAKER 1: So, you want a new school bag.
SPEAKER 2: **Yes, for my new school.**
SPEAKER 1: How big do you want it?
SPEAKER 2: **This big – like my old bag.**
SPEAKER 1: And, what colour?
SPEAKER 2: **Green or blue, please.**
SPEAKER 1: What about this bag? Do you like it?
SPEAKER 2: **Yes, that's what I want.**

Listening text 2
SPEAKER 1: I like Cambridge.
SPEAKER 2: ...
SPEAKER 1: It's got lots of nice shops.
SPEAKER 2: ...
SPEAKER 1: And we can go on a boat on the river.
SPEAKER 2: ...

SPEAKER 1: Do you want to come again?
SPEAKER 2: ...

Key

Track 17

SPEAKER 1: I like Cambridge.
SPEAKER 2: **I think, it's very nice, too.**
SPEAKER 1: It's got lots of nice shops.
SPEAKER 2: **Super, I want a book and some new clothes.**
SPEAKER 1: And we can go on a boat on the river.
SPEAKER 2: **That's a good idea.**
SPEAKER 1: Do you want to come again?
SPEAKER 2: **Yes, but not this week.**

78 CD: ...
YOU:

☑ Yes, for my new school.
☐ No, I want a bag for my holidays.
☐ Do you have school bags?

CD: ...
YOU:

☐ My books are big.
☐ £ 35.00! That's a lot of money.
☑ This big – like my old bag.

CD: ...
YOU:

☐ I can paint it.
☐ Have you got more colours?
☑ Green or blue, please.

CD: ...
YOU:

☑ Yes, that's what I want.
☐ That's a green bag.
☐ This is my bag.

79 CD: …
YOU:
- [ ] I want to go home.
- [x] I think it's very nice, too.
- [ ] The café is nice.

CD: …
YOU:
- [ ] I don't like nice shops.
- [x] Super, I want a book and some new clothes.
- [ ] When can we go to the museum?

CD: …
YOU:
- [x] That's a good idea.
- [ ] We can go swimming.
- [ ] Where are the bikes?

CD: …
YOU:
- [ ] I want a new car.
- [x] Yes, but not this week.
- [ ] No, it's only open today.

Topic 22: Kim's party

Listening text 1

ZOE: Hi Anne. Listen. On Monday Darren and I are having a party for my sister, Kim.
ANNE: …
ZOE: No, she's got a new job.
ANNE: …
ZOE: She's working for a bank in America – New York, I think.
ANNE: …
ZOE: Me, too. But Anne, listen. We're having a party for her – a surprise. We're inviting lots of her friends. Can you and Dave come, too?
ANNE: …

ZOE: It's on Friday, next week.
ANNE: ...
ZOE: It's in the Red Cat Hotel in Richmond. It starts about 8.30.
ANNE: ...
ZOE: No problem. I can phone the hotel and book a room for you. Oh, and Anne, don't buy a present.
ANNE: ...
ZOE: Because she can't take a lot with her to America. See you next week. Bye.

Key

ZOE: Hi Anne. Listen. On Monday Darren and I are having a party for my sister, Kim.
ANNE: **Is it her birthday?**
ZOE: No, she's got a new job.
ANNE: **That's nice. – Where is it and what's she doing?**
ZOE: She's working for a bank in America – New York, I think.
ANNE: **That's super. I want to go there, too.**
ZOE: Me, too. But Anne, listen. We're having a party for her – a surprise. We're inviting lots of her friends. Can you and Dave come, too?
ANNE: **When is it?**
ZOE: It's on Friday, next week.
ANNE: **That's OK. Where is the party?**
ZOE: It's in the Red Cat Hotel in Richmond. It starts about 8.30.
ANNE: **Super. But we need a room for Friday and Saturday night in the hotel.**
ZOE: No problem. I can phone the hotel and book a room for you. Oh, and Anne, don't buy a present.
ANNE: **Why not?**
ZOE: Because she can't take a lot with her to America. See you next week. Bye.

Listening text 2

ZOE: Hello, is that the Red Cat Hotel?
MR WEST: Yes, it is. Simon West here. How can I help you?
ZOE: Hello Mr West, it's Zoe George here. It's about the party next week.
MR WEST: I remember, yes – Friday, next week.
ZOE: That's right.
MR WEST: Is there a problem?
ZOE: No, there isn't a problem but I've got a question. Two people want to stay at the hotel on Friday and Saturday night. Is that possible?

MR WEST: That's no problem. I just need some details. OK, so the room is for 14th and 15th April ... and the names and addresses of the people are?
ZOE: Anne and Dave Black – 25 London Road, Aberdeen.
MR WEST: Anne and Dave Black – good. Have you got their phone number?
ZOE: It's 06832 / 88621.
MR WEST: OK, that's everything I need.
ZOE: Thank you. Bye.

80
(to) invite	**einladen**
(to) book	**buchen**
(to) stay	**übernachten**
possible	**möglich**
details	*(hier)* **Angaben**
address	**Adresse**

81
a) Here's my **address** – 14 Castle Street, Leeds.
b) I want to **stay** in a nice hotel in New York.
c) Can I **invite** Petra to our party?
d) Can you **book** a hotel room for me, please?
e) I want a large hotel room. Is that **possible**?
f) Can you give me your **details** for the hotel – your name, address and phone number?

82 ZOE: *Hi Anne. ...*
YOU: [✓] Is it her birthday?
[ ] How old is she?
[ ] Which sister?
ZOE: *No, ...*
YOU: [ ] That's terrible.
[ ] What time is it?
[✓] That's nice. – Where is it and what's she doing?
ZOE: *She's ...*

You: ☑ That's super. I want to go there, too.
☐ America? That's far away.
☐ Has she got a house there?

Zoe: *Me, ...*

You: ☐ What time is it?
☑ When is it?
☐ How big is the party?

Zoe: *It's ...*

You: ☐ Is the party at your house?
☐ That's a problem.
☑ That's OK. Where is the party?

Zoe: *It's ...*

You: ☑ Super. But we need a room for Friday and Saturday night in the hotel.
☐ Can we get breakfast in the hotel?
☐ Super. Is there a disco?

Zoe: *No ...*

You: ☐ That's great!
☐ What does she want?
☑ Why not?

Zoe: *Because ...*

Key – Words and Spelling | 227

83

Red Cat Hotel
Reservation form

Name(s): **Anne and Dave / David Black**

Address: **25, London Road, Aberdeen**

Number of nights: **2**   Date(s): **14th and 15th April**

Arrive on: **14th April**

Leave on: **16th April**

Phone number: **06832 / 88621**

Words and Spelling

Topic 23: School and the classroom

Listening 1
blackboard – chair – table – desk – notice board

Listening 2
Spelling in English – *Buchstabieren auf Englisch*
a – b – c – d – e – f – g – h – i – j – k – l – m – n –
o – p – q – r – s – t – u – v – w – x – y – z

Listening 3
- Most long rulers are 30 cms and most small rulers are 15 cms.
  R U L E R – ruler

- You can draw with a pencil.
  P E N C I L – pencil
- If you don't like what you write in pencil, you can use a rubber to start again.
  R U B B E R – rubber
- You use a paintbrush to paint pictures.
  P A I N T B R U S H – paintbrush
- You put your pens, pencils, ruler and scissors into a pencil case.
  P E N C I L C A S E – (2 words) pencil case
- You write with a pen.
  P E N – pen
- Pencil crayons are pencils with different colours.
  P E N C I L C R A Y O N – (2 words) pencil crayon
- A lot of pupils have got felt pens. These are pens with different colours.
  F E L T P E N – (2 words) felt pen
- You use a pair of scissors to cut paper.
  S C I S S O R S – a pair of scissors

84

85

A	rubber	B	ruler
C	pencil case	D	pencil crayon
E	paintbrush	F	felt pen
G	pen	H	pencil
I	(a pair of) scissors		

86 Jenny has got **three** pencil crayons, **two felt pens**, **a paintbrush**, **a pair of scissors** and **a pen**. But she hasn't got **a rubber**, **a pencil** or **a ruler**.

87

Topic 24: House, home and garden

Listening 1
chimney – door – doorbell – doorstep – roof – wall – window

Listening 2
to brush – to clean – to close – to open – to ring

Listening 3
downstairs – upstairs – dining room – bathroom – hall – bedroom – kitchen – landing – living room – toilet – stairs

Listening 4
- armchair – a r m c h a i r – armchair
- bed – b e d – bed
- carpet – c a r p e t – carpet
- chair – c h a i r – chair
- cupboard – c u p b o a r d – cupboard
- desk – d e s k – desk
- lamp – l a m p – lamp
- light – l i g h t – light
- bookshelf – b o o k s h e l f – bookshelf
  (plural) bookshelves – b o o k s h e l v e s – bookshelves
- sofa – s o f a – sofa
- wardrobe – w a r d r o b e – wardrobe

Listening 5
Here is Grandma's armchair. It's in the bathroom! Put it in her room downstairs.

James's wardrobe is in the living room. Please put it in the small bedroom for him.

Karen has got a nice bed, but it's in the kitchen. Can you put it in her room? It's next to James's.

George has got a new lamp for his bedroom, but it's in the toilet!

Look! There is Mr Smith's desk. It's in the dining room. He wants it in the living room.

Mr and Mrs Smith love their kitchen but not with their bedroom carpet in it. That's for their room.

Listening 6
bush – flower – grass – hedge – pond – tree –
drive – fence – garage – gate – path – shed

88 a) chimney   **Kamin, Schornstein**   b) door   **Tür**
     c) doorbell   **(Tür-)Klingel**   d) doorstep   **(Tür-)Schwelle**
     e) roof   **Dach**   f) wall   **Mauer, Wand**
     g) window   **Fenster**

89 a) 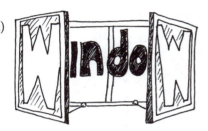 b)

90

91 a) brushing a doorstep   b) cleaning a window
     c) closing a door / a window   d) opening a door / a window
     e) ringing a doorbell

92 a) Sam **is cleaning the window.**
b) Mrs Jones **is closing the front door.**
c) Mandy **is ringing the doorbell / Tommy's doorbell.**
d) Kim **is opening the window.**
e) Fred **is brushing the doorstep.**
f) George **is closing the window.**
g) Rover **is opening the back door.**

93 a)

b) *individuelle Lösungen (für die Benennung der Räume vgl. 93 a).*

94 a) armchair   b) bed   c) carpet
d) chair   e) cupboard f) desk
g) lamp   h) light   i) (book)shelves (singular: shelf)
j) sofa   k) wardrobe

95 a)

name	object	wrong room (✗)	right room (✓)
Grandma	armchair	bathroom	her room
James	wardrobe	living room	small bedroom
Karen	bed	kitchen	her bedroom
George	lamp	toilet	his bedroom
Mr Smith	desk	dining room	living room
Mr & Mrs Smith	(bedroom) carpet	kitchen	their bedroom

b)

96
a) Busch
b) Blume
c) Gras
d) Hecke
e) Teich
f) Baum
g) Auffahrt
h) Zaun
i) Garage
j) Tor
k) Weg
l) Schuppen

97

98 a)

a flower (noun)   [flaʊə]

plural: two flowers

example: Roses are nice flowers.

to pick flowers (verb)

Blume

Plural: Blumen

Beispiel: Rosen sind schöne Blumen.

Blumen pflücken (Verb)

b)

grass (noun)   [grɑ:s]

no plural!

example: The grass is green.

(to) walk on the grass (verb)

Key – Words and Spelling 235

```
Gras
Plural?


Beispiel: Das Gras ist grün.
auf dem Gras laufen (Verb)
```

House	1	2	3	4	5	6	7	8
Name	Jenny	Anne	Jane	Mary	James	Mike	Bob	Peter

Topic 25: Colours

Listening 1
Track 30
black – blue – brown – green – grey – orange – purple – red – white – yellow

Listening 2
Track 31
Have you got your pencil crayons? Okay. Then listen carefully.
The sun is green and the sky is red.
There are two hands. The hands are black.
There are also two buildings. The big building is blue and the windows are yellow. The small building is orange and its windows are grey.
Now the last part of the picture – the hills. The hills are purple.

102 *mögliche Bilder:*
blau *(blue)*: Wasser, Meer
braun *(brown)*: Bär, Holz
schwarz *(black)*: Katze, Nacht
grau *(grey)*: Esel, Maus
orange *(orange)*: Orange
gelb *(yellow)*: Sonne, Zitrone
weiß *(white)*: Gespenst, Schnee
grün *(green)*: Blätter, Frosch
rot *(red)*: Tomate, Ampel
lila *(purple)*: Pflaume, Aubergine

103
a) green
c) red
e) brown
g) white
i) blue
b) yellow
d) red / yellow / green
f) black
h) purple

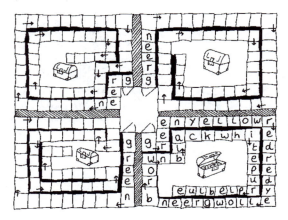

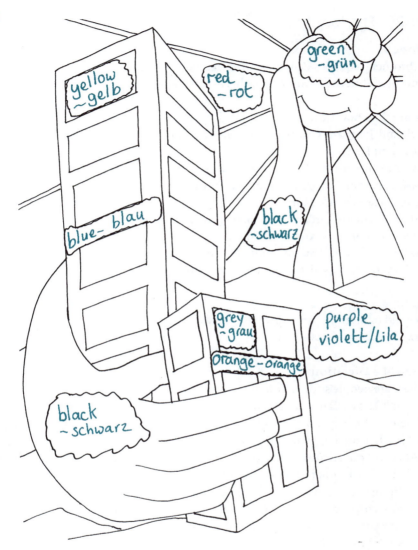

Topic 26: The family

Listening 1
aunt – brother – cousin – daughter – dad (father) – grandad (grandfather) – grandma (grandmother) – mum (mother) – sister – son – uncle

Listening 2 – Dictation
a) Mick and John are visiting their aunt and uncle, but Kim is watching TV with Aunt Jean.
b) SAM: Are you visiting Uncle Tom, today?
   MUM: Yes, I am. I'm giving your cousins these books.
c) JACKIE: Dad, where's Mum?
   DAD: She's in the garden. She's talking to your uncle.
d) MR SMITH: Karen, is your father there?
   KAREN: No, he isn't. But my mum is here.
   MR SMITH: Can I speak to your mother then?

Listening 3
baby – child (children) – grandparents – husband – nephew – niece – parents – wife

Listening 4 – Dictation
JO: Where are people sitting, Tom?
TOM: I don't know. Can you help me?
JO: Of course. Abi's grandparents can sit next to her. Her grandmother can sit on Abi's left and her grandfather on her right.
TOM: Abi's dad can sit next to her grandma and her mum next to her granddad.
JO: Put John, her brother, next to Abi's father and Karen, John's wife, next to Abi's mum. We can then put Abi's Uncle Martin, Aunt Jenny and her cousin, George, on the last three seats. George goes between his parents. Put Abi's aunt on George's right, next to John.
TOM: Haven't John and Karen got any children?
JO: Yes, they have, a boy and a girl. But Abi's nephew and niece can't come to the party.

Listening 5
friendly – funny – nice – old – pretty – small – tall – young

Key – Words and Spelling

106 individuelle Lösungen (vergleiche die Beschriftung mit den Begriffen in der Wörterliste zu Aufgabe 105)

107
a) Ian is David's **brother.**
b) Mary is David's **cousin.**
c) Lucy is David's **sister.**
d) Eric is Ian's **father / dad.**
e) Annie is Lucy's **grandmother / grandma.**
f) Nell is Margaret's **mother / mum.**
g) John is Ian's **grandfather / grandad.**
h) Karen is David's **aunt.**
i) Brian is Lucy's **uncle.**
j) Annie is Eric's **mother / mum.**

108
a) Mary / (Mary is Lucy's) cousin.
b) Ian and David / (Ian and David are Lucy's) brothers.
c) John / (John is Lucy's) grandfather.

109
a) Mick and John are visiting **their aunt and uncle,** but Kim is watching TV with **Aunt Jean.**
b) SAM: **Are you visiting Uncle Tom,** today?
   MUM: Yes, I am. I'm giving **your cousins these books.**
c) JACKIE: **Dad,** where's **Mum?**
   DAD: She's in the garden. She's talking to **your uncle.**
d) MR SMITH: Karen, is **your father there?**
   KAREN: No, he isn't. But **my mum is here.**
   MR SMITH: Can I speak to **your mother then?**

110

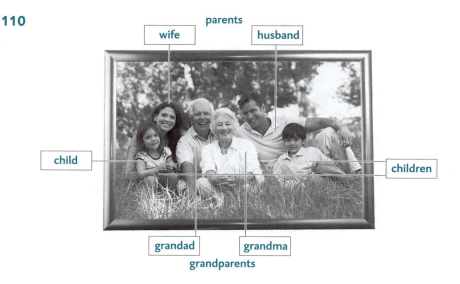

111 a) JO: Where are people sitting, Tom?
TOM: I don't know. Can you help me?
JO: Of course. Abi's **grandparents** can sit next to her. Her **grandmother** can sit on Abi's left and her **grandfather** on her right.
TOM: Abi's **dad** can sit next to her **grandma** and her **mum** next to her **grandad**.
JO: Put John, her **brother**, next to Abi's **father** and Karen, John's **wife**, next to Abi's **mum**. We can then put Abi's **Uncle Martin**, **Aunt Jenny** and her **cousin**, George, on the last three seats. George goes between his **parents**. Put Abi's **aunt** on George's right, next to John.
TOM: Haven't John and Karen got any children?
JO: Yes, they have – a boy and a girl. But Abi's **nephew** and **niece** can't come to the party.

b)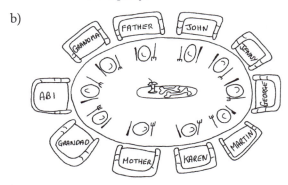

12

Großeltern	G	R	A	N	D	P	A	R	E	N	T	S
Tochter		D	A	U	G	H	T	E	R			
Kind					C	H	I	L	D			
Vati / Papa						D	A	D				
Bruder					B	R	O	T	H	E	R	
Cousine				C	O	U	S	I	N			
Sohn							S	O	N			
Ehemann			H	U	S	B	A	N	D			
Schwester						S	I	S	T	E	R	

13

friendly	funny	nice	old	pretty	small	tall	young
e	b	a	c	f	h	d	g
freundlich	lustig	nett	alt	hübsch	klein	groß	jung

14 a) Robert's grandfather is **old.**
b) Jenny's aunt is **tall.**
c) Kevin's uncle is **friendly / nice.**
d) William's brother is **funny.**
e) Jenny is **pretty.**
f) Roberta's sister is very **young.**
g) Norman's father is **small.**

Topic 27: Clothes

Listening 1
blouse – dress – (a pair of) jeans – pullover – shirt – (a pair of) shorts – skirt – (a pair of) socks – sweatshirt – tie – (a pair of) trousers – T-shirt

Listening 2
- You wear gloves on your hands. You can also say "a pair of gloves".
  gloves – G L O V E S – gloves
- Boys often wear caps on their heads.
  cap – C A P – cap

- A lot of people wear big coats in winter. Then they are very warm.
  coat – C O A T – coat
- A scarf is very long and you wear it around your neck. They often have nice colours.
  scarf – S C A R F – scarf
- Be careful when you have two scarves.
  The plural form is scarves – S C A R V E S – scarves
- A jacket is a short coat.
  jacket – J A C K E T – jacket
- You can also wear a hat on your head. There are lots of different hats. They don't all look like the hat in the picture.
  hat – H A T – hat

Listening 3 – Dictation

Track 39

a) I'm taking two suitcases. I've got five shirts, two pullovers, and one pair of trousers. Because it's warm, I'm taking two pairs of shorts. I've got three pairs of summer shoes, too. Hannah says we can swim in the sea so I've got two towels with me.

Track 40

b) Lewis always forgets things. I've got two towels for him so that we can go into the sea. I've got eight T-shirts, six pairs of shorts and my two pairs of sandals. My suitcase is full of clothes but I've got two books, too. One book is for me, it's called *The Nine Sea Monsters*, and I always get one book for Lewis, too. His book is about a very big shark.

115 a) Bluse   b) Kleid
c) Jeans   d) Pullover
e) Hemd   f) kurze Hose / Shorts
g) Rock   h) Socken / Kniestrümpfe
i) Sweatshirt   j) Krawatte
k) Hose   l) T-Shirt

116 a) Mr Peters is wearing a new pair of trousers.
b) Mrs Peters is wearing a new dress.
c) Tina is wearing a new sweatshirt / pullover.
d) Tom is wearing a new shirt.
e) Jake is wearing a new pair of socks.

17

A	B	C	D	E	F
cap	coat	hat	jacket	scarf pl.: scarves	(a pair of) gloves

18 *individuelle Lösungen*

19 a) Diktat vgl. *Listening Text* 3 a
b) Diktat vgl. *Listening Text* 3 b

20 *(Musterlösung)*
a) I am wearing a pair of jeans, a T-shirt and a sweatshirt. I'm wearing trainers, too.
b) I am wearing a pair of jeans, a hat, a pullover, a coat, a pair of gloves and a scarf.

21 a) The monkey has got **a jacket.**
b) The lion **has got a cap.**
c) The bear **has got (a pair of) gloves.**
d) The kangaroo **has got a coat.**
e) The elephant **has got a hat.**
f) The seal **has got a scarf.**

Topic 28: Animals and pets

Listening

- You get milk from a cow.
  cow – C O W – cow
- A bird flies.
  bird – B I R D – bird
- A mouse is very small and doesn't like cats. A mouse is also part of your computer.
  mouse – M O U S E – mouse
- You have to take a dog for a walk every day.
  dog – D O G – dog

- A lot of girls like horses. They ride them.
  horse – H O R S E – horse
- A sheep is often white. Sheep give us wool. We use the wool for pullovers.
  sheep – S H E E P – sheep
- A frog is often green and lives in water.
  frog – F R O G – frog
- Cats are clever but they chase small animals. A mouse doesn't like a cat.
  cat – C A T – cat
- A pig lives on a farm. It is often pink.
  pig – P I G – pig

122 a) bird   b) cat   c) cow
        d) dog   e) frog   f) horse
        g) mouse   h) pig   i) sheep

123 a) Noel is feeding a big **bird.**
        b) Julie **is going** to her **horse.**
        c) Michael **is swimming** with the **frogs.**
        d) Tina is looking for the **mouse / mice (plural)**.
        e) George is milking a **cow.**
        f) James **is carrying / is wearing** a bag with a **sheep** on it.
        g) Linda **is walking** with her **dog.**
        h) Chris **is wearing** a **pig's** mask.
        i) Vicky **is playing** with her **cat.**

24 a)

mouse	Maus
bird	Vogel
frog	Frosch
horse	Pferd
sheep	Schaf
dog	Hund
cow	Kuh
cat	Katze

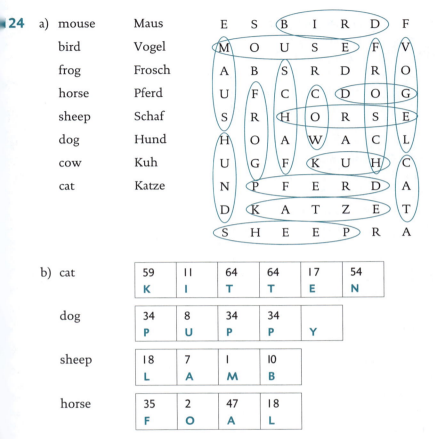

b)

cat

59	11	64	64	17	54
K	I	T	T	E	N

dog

34	8	34	34		
P	U	P	P	Y	

sheep

18	7	1	10
L	A	M	B

horse

35	2	47	18
F	O	A	L

25 *individuelle Lösungen*

Topic 29: The body

Listening 1
arm – back – chest – foot (pl. feet) – finger – hand – head – knee – leg – neck – thumb

Listening 2
broken   I have got a broken leg.
cold   She has got a cold.

headache	He has got a headache.
(to) hurt	Her arm hurts.
(to) feel ill	Andrew feels ill.
sore	Mary has got a sore finger.
swollen	Peter has got a swollen arm.
toothache	Mrs Smith has got toothache.

Listening 3

RECEPTIONIST: Good afternoon, Doctor.
DOCTOR: Good afternoon, Rita. Who wants to see me this afternoon?
RECEPTIONIST: Six people – but I'm sorry, they aren't on a list.
DOCTOR: No problem. I can write the list.
RECEPTIONIST: Okay. Mrs Green is at 3 o'clock – she's got a headache. Then we've got Mr George – he thinks he's got a broken finger. He's at half past three. Julie Peters is coming at half past two because her back hurts. At a quarter past four we have Karen King. She's got a swollen leg. Before her at 4 o'clock James Black is coming with a sore chest. And, then there's Mr Bell with a bad cold – he's at a quarter to three.
DOCTOR: Thank you, Rita.

Listening 4 – Dictation

MR LONDON: Hello, my name is Peter London. My knee hurts and it's swollen. Can I see the doctor please?
RECEPTIONIST: Of course, please sit over there.
MISS RICHARDS: I'm Becky Richards. I've got a problem with my arm. It hurts when I move it. I don't think it is broken.
RECEPTIONIST: Wait over there, please.
MRS BIRD: I feel very ill. Can I see the doctor, please? I've got a bad cold and a headache, too. I've also got toothache. My back and my chest are also sore. I feel terrible. My name is Susan Bird.
RECEPTIONIST: Oh dear. You can see the doctor next. Sit over there, please, outside her door.

126 a) Arm   b) Rücken   c) Brust
       d) Fuß/Füße   e) Finger   f) Hand
       g) Kopf   h) Knie   i) Bein
       j) Nacken/Hals k) Daumen

128 a) Jenny has got a **broken finger.** b) Mike's hand **hurts / is swollen.**
c) Peter has got a **cold.** d) Mandy's got **toothache.**
e) Robert has got a **headache.** f) Georgina has got a **swollen foot.**
g) Ken has got a **sore knee.**

129

time	name	illness *(Krankheit)*
2.30	Julie Peters	back hurts
2.45	Mr Bell	bad cold
3.00	Mrs Green	headache
3.15	–	–
3.30	Mr George	broken finger
3.45	–	–
4.00	James Black	sore chest
4.15	Karen King	swollen leg

30 MR LONDON: Hello, My name is Peter London. **My knee hurts and it's swollen. Can I see the doctor please?**
RECEPTIONIST: Of course, please sit over there.
MISS RICHARDS: **I'm Becky Richards. I've got a problem with my arm. It hurts when I move it. I don't think it is broken.**
RECEPTIONIST: Wait over there, please.
MRS BIRD: **I feel very ill. Can I see the doctor, please? I've got a bad cold and a headache, too. I've also got toothache. My back and my chest are also sore. I feel terrible. My name is Susan Bird.**
RECEPTIONIST: **Oh dear. You can see the doctor next. Sit over there, please, outside this door.**

131

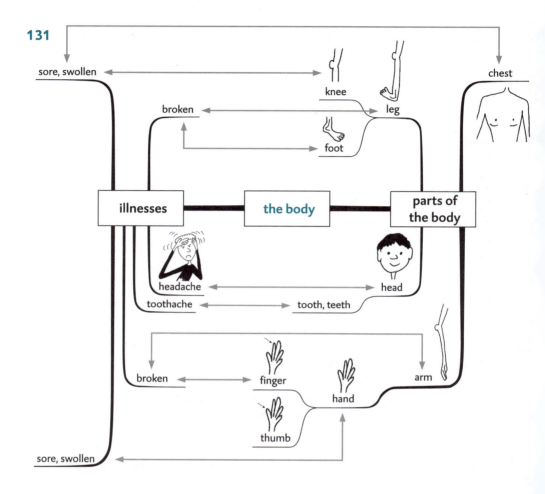

Topic 30: British or American English?

Track 46

Listening 1

MARKUS: Hello, Jessica. Hello, Rachel.
JESSICA: Hello, Markus. It's nice to see you again. How are you?
MARKUS: Fine, thanks. But I've got a problem and maybe you two can help me.
RACHEL: What's the problem, Markus?
MARKUS: Well you both speak English but you've got different words for some things. Like … I know – in German we have *Handys*.
RACHEL: A *Handy (laughs)*! You mean a mobile.
JESSICA: No, no, no. Markus means a cell phone.

MARKUS: Exactly. There are two words for my *Handy* – one American and one British.
JESSICA: Let me think of another word. I know. I like fries. And you Rachel?
RACHEL: Chips! Lovely, big, fat chips! And you Markus?
MARKUS: I like *Pommes*!
JESSICA: This is fun – OK – I walk on the sidewalk.
RACHEL: I walk on the pavement – and … Markus? What do you walk on?
MARKUS: *Ich gehe auf dem Bürgersteig!*

Listening 2
JESSICA: Americans spell color, harbor and neighbor without a "u".
RACHEL: That's right. In Britain we spell harbour – h a r b o u r.
JESSICA: And in America it's h a r b o r.
MARKUS: Excuse me, I know what colour and neighbour mean but what's a harbour?
RACHEL: In German it's a *Hafen*, Markus.
JESSICA: We also spell "center" and "jewelry" differently.
RACHEL: Yes, you do. In Britain centre is c e n t r e and jewellery is j e w e l l e r y. And Markus, don't ask – jewellery is *Schmuck*.
MARKUS: I knew that, Rachel. But how do you spell "centre" and "jewellery" in American English?
JESSICA: That's easy – c e n t e r and j e w e l r y.
MARKUS: I've got another question – do you two understand each other?
RACHEL: Of course! We both speak English, don't we?

32 a)

German	American English	British English
Handy	cell phone	mobile (phone)
Pommes	fries	chips
Bürgersteig	sidewalk	pavement

b)

German	American English	British English
Farbe	color	colour
Hafen	harbor	harbour
Nachbar	neighbor	neighbour
Zentrum	center	centre
Schmuck	jewelry	jewellery

133 a) A.E.: He walks along the sidewalk talking to his friend on his **cell phone.**
B.E.: He walks along the **pavement** talking to his friend on his mobile.

b) A.E.: "I like the **color** of your neighbor's car," says Julie.
B.E.: "I like the colour of your **neighbour's** car," says Julie.

c) A.E.: The **sidewalk** in the town center is new.
B.E.: The pavement in the town **centre** is new.

d) A.E.: The café next to the jewelry shop sells great fries.
B.E.: The café next to the **jewellery** shop sells great **chips.**

e) A.E.: Can I use your cell phone to phone my friend at the **harbor**, please?
B.E.: Can I use your **mobile (phone)** to phone my friend at the harbour, please?

134

	USA or UK?	key word
A	UK	chips
B	USA	sidewalk
C	USA	cell phone
D	USA	center
E	USA	harbor, fries
F	UK	jewellery
G	UK	centre

Mediation

Topic 31: A visit to Norfolk

35 a) ☐ Ihr müsst weiterfahren, weil man nicht auf dem Gras parken darf. Hunde müssen an die Leine.

☑ Autos sollen auf dem Gras geparkt werden. Der Ausgang ist geradeaus. Wenn ihr einen Hund habt, muss er angeleint sein.

☐ Du musst mit deinem Hund diesen Ausgang nehmen. Man soll auf dem Gras parken.

b) VATER: Wo können wir denn hier parken? Ich kann nirgends einen Parkplatz sehen.
DU: **Du kannst auf dem Gras / der Wiese / dem Rasen parken.**
VATER: Soll ich dann geradeaus fahren?
DU: **Nein, du kannst hier parken. Geradeaus ist der Ausgang. / Geradeaus geht es zum Ausgang.**
MUTTER: Sollen wir den Hund besser im Auto lassen?
DU: Nein, wir können **ihn mitnehmen, aber er muss an die Leine.**

36 a) Mama, darf ich mir ein Eis kaufen? / soll ich Eis für uns alle kaufen? Hier rechts ist gleich eine Eisdiele.

b) VATER: Ich habe jetzt keine Lust auf Eis. Wollen wir nicht lieber etwas „Richtiges" essen?
DU: **Wir können hier etwas essen, im „The Buttery".**
VATER: Was ist *The Buttery*?
DU: **„The Buttery" ist / Das ist ein Café. / Ein Café.**
MUTTER: Kannst du uns sagen, was auf dem Schild steht?
DU: **Kein Problem, das ist die Speisekarte. Es gibt Baguettes, Paninis (ich weiß nicht, was Paninis sind, wisst ihr das?), Suppe, Salat, Kartoffeln, Bagels (was ist das nun wieder?), Kuchen und Eis. Sie bieten außerdem den ganzen Tag lang Frühstück an.**
VATER: Klingt gut, aber hoffentlich dauert das nicht zu lange. Wir wollen doch noch spazieren gehen. Was meinst du?
DU: **Wir müssen nicht unbedingt im Café essen, wir können auch etwas zum Mitnehmen kaufen.**

137

Holkham Hall ist im Juli sonntags, montags, dienstags und donnerstags von 12 bis 16 Uhr geöffnet. Das passt, heute ist ja Donnerstag. Wir müssen nur noch eine halbe Stunde warten. Aber am 18. und 19. Juli ist geschlossen. (Welches Datum ist denn heute?)

Der Eintritt kostet für Erwachsene 8 £ und für Kinder 4 £. (Es gibt auch noch einen Familienpreis, aber wenn wir nur das Schloss sehen wollen, lohnt sich das nicht.) Du kannst die Eintrittskarten hier an der Kasse kaufen.

Topic 32: Can you help me? I don't speak German.

138 Between **1st April** and **15th October** you can **go into / get into / enter** the **tower every day** until **7 p.m. / 7 o'clock in the evening.**

39

We can go on a boat around the harbour / have a tour of the harbour. It costs € 9 for adults and € 4.50 for children. / We are children, we must pay € 4.50. The next tour is at 2 p.m. / We can take the boat at 2 p.m.

40
a)

b) "Schloss am See" is a <u>wildlife park</u>. You can walk in the park and you can <u>feed</u> the animals. There are <u>birds of prey shows</u>, too. There is also a children's <u>playground</u>. You can get something to eat and drink at the café.
In the summer "Schloss am See" is open from 9.30 a.m. to 8 p.m.
It costs € 9,50 for adults. How old is your child? Children under 5 are free.

Topic 33: The country teenager

141   a) Der Text handelt von Amy, einem Mädchen, das in einem kleinen Dorf wohnt. Amy erzählt von ihrem täglichen Leben. / Sie erzählt aus ihrem Alltag.

b) In Amys Dorf gibt es keinen Schulbus, daher muss sie jeden Morgen (an Schultagen) zum Bahnhof laufen. Er ist etwa 20 Minuten von ihrem Haus entfernt. Bei schlechtem Wetter fährt ihr Vater sie dorthin. Sie nimmt dann den (Regional-)Zug in die Stadt, wo sich die Schule befindet / wo die Schule ist. Sie muss noch einmal fünfzehn Minuten zu Fuß gehen bis sie zur Schule kommt. Dabei muss sie einen Berg hinauflaufen.

c) Sie sieht ihre Freunde in der Schule und, wenn sie zu Hause ist, bleibt sie durch Internet und Handy in Kontakt / geht sie ins Internet oder schreibt SMS.

d) Es ist ziemlich schwierig für sie, Popgruppen live zu sehen, weil sie weit zu den Konzerten fahren muss. Die nächste Konzerthalle ist 90 Minuten entfernt.

Topic 34: My London walk

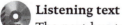
Listening text
The next bus tour around the city is at 4.30. You can buy tickets on the bus. The tour is £ 7.50 for adults and £ 5 for children. The tour is for 90 minutes. The bus goes past fifteen famous London sights – for example, Big Ben, Buckingham Palace and the Tower of London.

142   Toni is **writing** about **a walk in / through / around** London. She wants to tell her **friend** about **the walk** because **he / her friend** is going to **visit London**, too.

43 Of course, I can help you. For me, the centre / middle of London is Trafalgar Square. You can go shopping in Oxford Street and Regent Street. There are lots of shops. There is an area of London called Mayfair. Mayfair is where many rich people live. / Many rich people live in Mayfair.

44 Die nächste Stadtrundfahrt beginnt um 16:30 Uhr. Sie können das Ticket im Bus kaufen; es kostet 7,50 £. Die Tour dauert 90 Minuten und der Bus fährt an 15 der berühmtesten Sehenswürdigkeiten Londons vorbei. (Zum Beispiel an Big Ben, Buckingham Palace oder dem Tower.)

45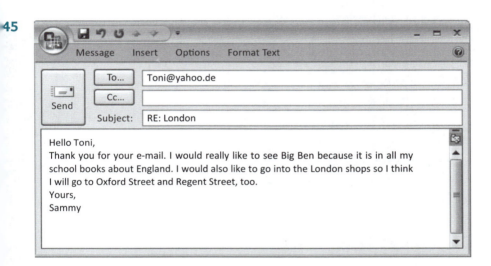

46 a)

1	2	3	4	5
B	A	D	C	E

b)

A	Trafalgar Square is the centre of London for me.
B	I take the Underground to Trafalgar Square.
C	Lots of famous (rich) people stay in this big hotel.
D	This is the way to Buckingham Palace. / St. James park. / a park in London.
E	There are lots of shops in Oxford Street.

Topic 35: Sorry, I don't understand!

147 KIM: Where's Sophia, Dave? Oh, there she is. Sophia! Sophia! Come here – quick! I don't understand what the woman is saying.
KELLNERIN: *Was möchtet ihr?*
SOPHIA: She wants to know … ☐ what time it is.
　　　　　　　　　　　　　　☒ what you would like.
　　　　　　　　　　　　　　☐ do you like him?
KIM: A glass of water, please.
DAVE: And a large cola for me.
SOPHIA: ☒ *Sie möchte ein Glas Wasser und er möchte eine große Cola.*
　　　　 ☐ *Er möchte ein Wasser und sie möchte eine Cola.*
　　　　 ☐ *Sie möchte eine Flasche Wasser und eine Cola.*
KELLNERIN: *Möchte sie ein großes Glas Wasser oder ein kleines?*
SOPHIA: ☐ How do you want the water?
　　　　 ☒ Do you want a large or a small glass of water?
　　　　 ☐ Is his water big or small?
KIM: A large glass of water, please.
DAVE: And, can I have some ice in my drink?
SOPHIA: ☐ *Ein großes Glas Wasser mit Eiswürfeln.*
　　　　 ☐ *Die Getränke mit Eiswürfeln.*
　　　　 ☒ *Ein großes Glas Wasser und Eiswürfel in der Cola.*

148 ROBIN: *Mein Freund will ein Geschenk für seine Mutter kaufen.*
VERKÄUFER: *Was möchte er denn für sie kaufen?*
ROBIN: **What do you want for her / your mum?**
DAVE: I'd like some chocolates. But I don't have a lot of money.
ROBIN: **Mein Freund möchte Schokolade. Aber er hat nicht viel Geld.**
VERKÄUFER: *Bei diesen hier kosten 100 Gramm nur 6,35 €.*
ROBIN: **These are only € 6.35 for 100 grams.**
DAVE: € 6.35!! I only have € 4. Can I buy anything for € 4?
ROBIN: **Er hat nur 4 €. Kann er irgendetwas für 4 € kaufen?**
VERKÄUFER: *Leider nicht. Aber der Supermarkt dort hat auch Schokolade.*

ROBIN: **No, you can't. But you can go to the supermarket over there. They have got chocolates, too.**
DAVE: Can we go there, now?

49 VERKÄUFERIN: *Kann ich euch helfen?*
SOPHIA: *Diese T-Shirts gefallen meiner Freundin.*
VERKÄUFERIN: *Welche Größe hat sie?*
SOPHIA: **What size are you?**
KIM: I usually need a small size.
SOPHIA: **Normalerweise eine kleine Größe / Größe S.**
VERKÄUFERIN: *Das ist ihre Größe. Sie kann es dort anprobieren.*
SOPHIA: **This is your size. You can try it on over there.**
KIM: It's the right size. Is there a blue one?
SOPHIA: **Es passt / Es ist die richtige Größe, aber haben Sie es auch in Blau?**
VERKÄUFERIN: *Nein, leider nicht. Wir haben diese T-Shirts nur in Weiß oder Grün. Soll ich sie euch zeigen?*
SOPHIA: **They only have them in white or green. Would you like to see them?**
KIM: Only the white T-shirt – I don't like green – and can you ask her how much the T-shirts are?
SOPHIA: **Nur das Weiße bitte (sie mag Grün nicht). Wie viel kosten sie / die T-Shirts?**
VERKÄUFERIN: *Sie kosten 25 €.*
SOPHIA: **They cost € 25.**

Topic 36: Student exchange

Listening text 1
Here is a weather report on what's happening at the moment around England. In the north it's raining – so you need your umbrellas there today. In Cornwall it's very windy and cold. Sam from Plymouth says it's just starting to snow there. In the south-east of England it's also very cold but it's not raining in London, today. We hope to see some sun there after lunch, too.

Listening text 2
Track 50

I like my job. A lot of people think I do something unusual. I'm a bus driver but not a normal bus driver. I drive the bus for a very famous football team. I like driving my bus but I also like talking to the footballers. I stay in the same hotels, too. The only thing I don't like about my job is when my footballers lose.

Listening text 3
Track 51

This is Norwich. We're stopping here for two hours to go shopping and to have something to eat before we take you all back to the airport. We're in the middle of the city centre at the moment. As you can see, we're opposite the market. We meet here at 3 o'clock. Don't be late.
Most of the shops are in that area over there. You can see the main street from here. Walk along this road for 20 metres and then turn right. There are no cars in this area – it's for people only – so it's very safe. There are lots of shops and cafés along the main street and in the smaller streets on the left and the right.
When you walk around the town, stay in groups. If you need a teacher, phone us. We're in the Red Dog Café. That's in Tower Street – and our mobile phone numbers are on the list that you've got.
Have fun and remember – two hours only! Be here again at 3 o'clock.

Listening text 4
Track 52

Verehrte Fahrgäste, aufgrund einer Signalstörung am Bahnhof Würzburg wird der ICE 2012 nach Frankfurt Hauptbahnhof 30 Minuten verspätet eintreffen. Fahrplanmäßige Ankunft war 12:55, die neue Ankunftszeit ist 13:25. Wir bitten um Entschuldigung.

Listening text 5
Track 53

Guten Tag, meine Damen und Herren, ich begrüße die zugestiegenen Fahrgäste im ICE 2012 auf der Fahrt nach Frankfurt. Wir bedauern die Verspätung unseres Zuges. Über Ihre weiteren Verbindungen werde ich Sie kurz vor dem Bahnhof Frankfurt informieren. Wir möchten Sie darauf aufmerksam machen, dass der Speisewagen jetzt für Sie geöffnet ist. Wir können Ihnen heiße oder kalte Getränke anbieten und wir haben außerdem eine große Auswahl an Sandwiches und Kuchen. Der Speisewagen befindet sich im vorderen Zugteil, kurz vor den Wagen der ersten Klasse.

Listening text 6

Passagiere des Flugs Lufthansa LH2526 nach London Heathrow, bitte kommen Sie zu Gate 25. Das Gate ist jetzt geöffnet und Sie können in einigen Minuten einsteigen. Wir bitten die Passagiere der Sitzreihen 15–27 jetzt zum Gate zu kommen. Passagiere der Sitzreihen 1–14, bitte gedulden Sie sich noch einige Minuten, bis Sie von uns aufgerufen werden. Ihre Sitzreihe finden Sie auf Ihrer Bordkarte. Vielen Dank.

In Cornwall wird es heute sehr windig und kalt sein. Heute Nachmittag wird es in London kalt und trocken sein, vielleicht kommt aber noch die Sonne heraus.

Mary hat einen ungewöhnlichen Beruf. Sie ist die Busfahrerin einer berühmten Fußballmannschaft. Sie mag ihren Beruf, weil sie gerne Bus fährt und sich gerne mit den Spielern unterhält. Das Einzige was sie nicht mag ist, wenn ihre Mannschaft verliert.

a)

Why is the bus stopping?
to go shopping
to eat something

Where is the bus?
Norwich city centre, opposite the market

Meet – where? when?
at the bus, at 3 o'clock

Extra information
cafés and shops are in the main street and in the small streets left and right (safe, no cars)
we have to stay in groups

Problems?
teachers are in the Red Dog Café (Tower Street); their phone numbers are on the list

b) Der Bus hält hier in Norwich, damit wir etwas essen und auch einkaufen gehen können. Wir sind hier in der Stadtmitte, gegenüber ist der Markt. Wir treffen uns um 15 Uhr wieder hier. Dort drüben ist die Hauptstraße,

das ist eine Fußgängerzone. In der Hauptstraße und in den Seitenstraßen gibt es viele Geschäfte und Cafés. Wir müssen in Gruppen bleiben.
Falls wir Probleme haben, können wir die Lehrer anrufen. Hast du noch die Liste mit den Telefonnummern? Sie sind im Red Dog Café in der Tower Street. (Pünktlich in zwei Stunden sollen wir zurück sein, das hat sie mehrmals gesagt ...)

153 a) Our **train** is **30 minutes** late.

b) **Yes, you can.** You can **buy** hot and cold **drinks, sandwiches and cakes** near the front of **the train.**

c) We have to go to **Gate 25**. Because we sit **in Row 14** we must **wait** until the other **passengers / people** in **Rows 15–27** get onto the **plane.**

Topic 37: School project

Listening text 1

Track 55

SCHÜLER: Frau Schmidt, dürfen wir Ihnen ein paar Fragen stellen? Es ist für unser Projekt mit der Partnerschule in Ohio.
FRAU SCHMIDT: Ja, natürlich.
SCHÜLER: Können Sie bitte etwas über sich selbst erzählen?
FRAU SCHMIDT: Hm, wo soll ich da anfangen? Ich bin 29 Jahre alt, ich unterrichte Englisch und Deutsch – aber das wisst ihr ja sicher. Ich komme aus Karlsruhe.
SCHÜLER: Sind Sie verheiratet?
FRAU SCHMIDT: Ja, mein Mann ist Pilot. Kinder haben wir noch keine.
SCHÜLER: Was machen Sie denn in ihrer Freizeit?
FRAU SCHMIDT: Was ist Freizeit? *(lacht)* Spaß beiseite. Ich mag viele Dinge – ins Kino gehen oder meine Freunde treffen. Ich lese gerne und höre auch gerne Musik. Und ich gehe gerne mit Ben laufen.
SCHÜLER: Ist Ben ihr Mann?
FRAU SCHMIDT: *(lacht)* Nein, das ist Max – Ben ist mein Hund! Ein riesiger irischer Wolfshund, und der ist wirklich faul, deshalb laufen wir meistens auch nicht lange.
SCHÜLER: Können Sie auch noch andere Sprachen sprechen?
FRAU SCHMIDT: Ja, ich spreche auch Französisch.

SCHÜLER: Welche drei Dinge würden Sie gerne mit auf eine einsame Insel nehmen?
FRAU SCHMIDT: Ein gutes Buch, mein Smartphone und Ben.
SCHÜLER: Nicht Ihren Mann?
FRAU SCHMIDT: Der würde nicht mitkommen – auf einsamen Inseln können keine Flugzeuge landen!

Listening text 2
YOU: Hello, Chelsea, it's Annalena from Germany.
CHELSEA: Hello, Annalena. It's nice to hear from you. Are you phoning about the project?
YOU: Yes, I am. Can you answer lots of questions for me?
CHELSEA: Sure.
YOU: Can you tell me something about where you live?
CHELSEA: Yeah, OK. I live in Santa Barbara – that's 'Santa' like in Santa Claus and then the girl's name, 'Barbara'. It's a nice town, most houses here are white and we've got lots of palm trees. It's often nice and warm and sunny here, too. Santa Barbara is a town but it's not very big. It's on the Pacific coast, so there's a nice beach, too.
YOU: That's super. Do you live in a house or a flat?
CHELSEA: My family have got a house. We live near the beach. My friends and I often go swimming there. Or sometimes we play volleyball on the beach.
YOU: What's your school like?
CHELSEA: Big. American schools are often big; we've got about 2000 pupils. Many pupils come by bus to our school from the villages near Santa Barbara. Oh, before I forget – I have to ask you some questions, too. Can I phone you on Saturday?
YOU: Saturday is OK – and thank you for all the information.
CHELSEA: Anytime. Bye.

154 a)

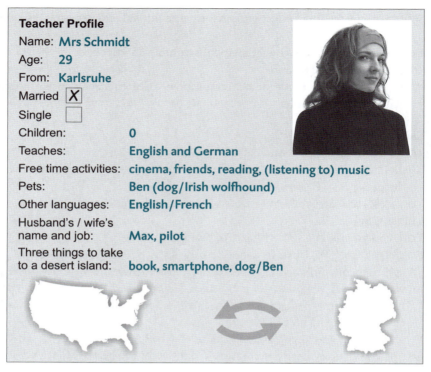

Teacher Profile
Name: **Mrs Schmidt**
Age: **29**
From: **Karlsruhe**
Married **X**
Single ☐
Children: **0**
Teaches: **English and German**
Free time activities: **cinema, friends, reading, (listening to) music**
Pets: **Ben (dog/Irish wolfhound)**
Other languages: **English/French**
Husband's / wife's name and job: **Max, pilot**
Three things to take to a desert island: **book, smartphone, dog/Ben**

b) Mrs Schmidt teaches English and German. She is 29 years old and comes from Karlsruhe. She is married. Her husband's name is Max and he is a pilot. They haven't got children. She likes going to the cinema, meeting friends, reading and listening to music. She has got a big dog. She would take a good book, her smartphone and her dog, Ben, to the desert island.

c)

School Project: Task 2	Notes about Chelsea
Phone your American partner. Find out about where he/she lives. Tell your class tomorrow about your partner **in German**. Good luck!	– Wohnort: Santa Barbara, kleinere Stadt am Pazifik, weiße Häuser, Palmen, Strand, schönes Wetter – lebt in einem Haus in Strandnähe – Hobbies: Schwimmen, Beachvolleyball – Schule: sehr groß (2000 Schüler)

d) Meine amerikanische Freundin heißt Chelsea und wohnt in Santa Barbara. Die Häuser dort sind weiß gestrichen und es gibt viele Palmen. Normalerweise ist das Wetter in Santa Barbara sehr schön – warm und sonnig. Santa

Barbara ist eine Stadt an der Pazifikküste und hat natürlich einen Strand. Chelsea wohnt in einem Haus in der Nähe des Strands. Sie und ihre Freunde schwimmen oft im Meer oder spielen Beachvolleyball. Wie in den USA üblich, ist Chelseas Schule sehr groß. Viele der 2000 Schüler kommen aus kleineren Orten in der Nähe von Santa Barbara.

Writing

Topic 38: Land's End

55 a) The date in the photo is **17th August 2009.**
    b) It is **3147** miles to New York.
    c) There are **three** people near the signpost.
    d) The **woman** in the white T-shirt is **putting** letters on the signpost.
    e) The other people are **watching** her. / … **standing and watching** her.
    f) I think it is a **warm / sunny / nice** day.
    g) I can **see** the sea behind the **signpost.**

56 a) I think this place is called Land's End because **it is the end of England. (… it is the last place in England.)**
    b) I can put **my town and the date / how far / how many miles it is from Land's End on the signpost.**

57 a)

Hintergrund (background):
family (woman, two children), people, houses, road

T-shirt text:
Land's End to John o'Groats 1000 miles

Vordergrund (foreground):
three men; they are cycling

Wetter (weather), Jahreszeit (season):
warm, sunshine; maybe spring or summer

Ort (place):
road in the country (auf dem Land)

b) BOY: Where are you cycling to?
   YOU: **We are cycling to John o'Groats.**
   BOY: Where is John o'Groats?
   YOU: **John o'Groats / It is in Scotland.**
   BOY: How many miles is it to John o'Groats?
   YOU: **It is 1000 miles to John o'Groats.**
   BOY: Where are your bags?
   YOU: **They are in a friend's car.**

c)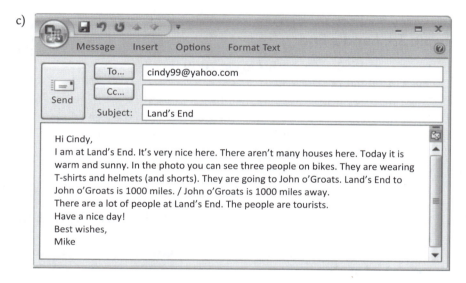

Topic 39: Fiona from Scotland

158 a) **Fiona** has got a **brother** and a **sister.**
   b) Her brother's **name** is **Andrew**. Her **sister's** name **is** Lilly.
   c) They **live** in a **house** in **Scotland.**

159 (*Musterlösung*)
   a) Fiona and Andrew's / Their school is in Edinburgh. / Andrew and Fiona / They go to school in Edinburgh.
   b) Fiona's favourite lesson is English and Andrew's favourite lesson is music.
   c) Their / The first lesson begins at 9 o'clock in the morning / at 9 a.m. and their last lesson ends at 3.30 p.m.

60 Fiona goes to her **window** and **looks** outside. She **sees** a woman. The woman is **walking** away from her **house**. Fiona goes to the front **door**, she **opens** it and there she **finds** a big box **with** her name on it. On the box there are the **words** 'Happy Birthday, Fiona'. Fiona **likes** surprises and this really **is** a surprise.

61 Loch Ness is in Scotland. It **is** famous for its monster. The monster's name is Nessie. **Stories** about a monster in Loch Ness are not **new**. **One** story is **over** 1400 years old. This story is about a famous saint that **meets** a monster at Loch Ness.
The name "Nessie" isn't **old**. It is from a newspaper in 1933. There are photos of Nessie but they are **never** good photos. People **say** that Nessie has got a **long** neck and a hump.
What do you think? Is there a monster in Loch Ness?

Topic 40: I live here

62 a) Fiona's children **have got bikes.**
b) Zoe has got a **river**, a **bridge** and **three trees** in her garden.
c) Joe has got a **swimming pool** in his **garden**.
d) Peter lives between the house with **the tree (in the garden)** and the house with **the flowers (in the garden).**
e) Katie's house is opposite **the house with the bikes. / Fiona's house.**
f) Dr Charles lives **in the house with one tree in the garden.**
g) **Mrs Bruce has got a big car.**

63 *(Musterlösung)*
a) My house has got **ten** windows.
b) **My house has got a big garden.**
c) **The colour of my house is white. / My house is white.**
d) **The house opposite my house is very big.** It's green.

64 *(Musterlösung)*
The house in the photograph is white and it has got a chimney. Upstairs there is a big balcony. The house has also got a garage. The garage has got a white

door. The front door is next to the garage. I can see two or three windows. One window, I think, is also the door to the balcony. The house has got a small garden.

Topic 41: An e-mail to …

165 *(Musterlösung)*
a) I live in **Bergstraße in Neustadt.**
b) My favourite day is **Monday.**
c) My birthday is in **October.**
d) **The name of my favourite pop group is One Direction. / My favourite pop group is called One Direction.**
e) **Dear Mr and Mrs Woods,**
f) **My favourite book / film is "How to Train Your Dragon".**

166 a) The bookshop is in Green Lane.
b) It is Georgina's birthday. The present is from (her) Uncle Harry.
c) Mike comes from Scotland.

167 a)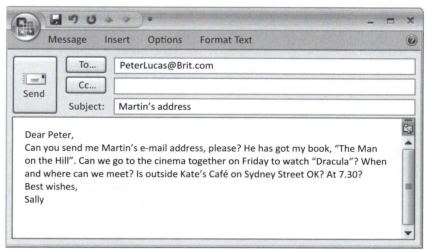

b)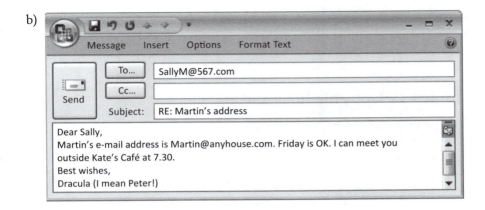

Topic 42: Some things just happen

68 a) There is a **small** window, over there.
b) He sees a **nice / small** bridge.
c) She works in a **flower** shop.
d) Carol has got **an old** car.
e) There is a **big** dog in the **nice** garden.

69 It is a warm and sunny day.
Lilly phones Kate. She asks her (friend) / Kate: "Do you want to play tennis?"
Lilly and Kate play tennis in the garden.
Lilly hits the ball and it breaks a window.
Lilly and Kate run away.

70 a) Cal's village is small and sometimes there's nothing to do there. Today, Cal's parents are working and his sister is playing outside. Cal **phones** his friend, Tony, and asks him to meet him at the bridge. At two o'clock, Tony is **at the bridge / waiting at the bridge / sitting on the bridge.**
"What can we do?" Cal asks Tony. "Let's go to the river," Tony answers.
After ten minutes the boys stop walking and **throw stones into the river.**
Suddenly, Cal sees something **in the river / in the water.**
"What's that, Tony? Over there. Can you see it?" Cal asks.
"There's nothing there, Cal," says Tony.
"I'm going to see what it is," Cal says. He **puts his hand** into the river and finds **a sword.**

b)

1	2	3	4	5	6
E	C	A	D	F	B

Topic 43: Happy birthday, Luke!

171 a) Today, it's (my friend) Luke's birthday.
b) He's 12 years old and has got lots of nice presents.
c) His sister Emma's present is a CD of rap hits.
d) (In the afternoon) he goes to the cinema (in town) with his best friends.
e) He has a very nice day.

172 It is **Luke's birthday** today. He has got **a skateboard** for **his (twelfth)** birthday.
He is happy with his **skateboard / present**.
He is **in the park (with his skateboard). He is having lots of fun.**
Now, **it is raining.**
Luke goes home and **opens his other presents / opens more presents.**

173

Music wish from:
Name: **Annie Carpenter**   From: **Edinburgh**
To:
Name: **Luke Scott**
Address: **5 Hill Road, Liverpool**
Why: **his 12th birthday**

Song / music type request: **rap song**
Message: **Happy birthday Luke! Sorry I'm not in Liverpool.**
Time for song: **7 o'clock (7 p.m. / early evening)**
Date: **16th March**

Topic 44: Free time

74 a)

Name	Carmen	Zhen	Chloe	Trevor	Eric	Dave
Photo	D	F	A	E	C	B
Word	canoeing	sight-seeing	horse riding	mountain biking	driving	surfing

b) **Carmen:** Carmen is 15 years old. She likes rivers and the sea. She enjoys canoeing.
Chloe: Chloe is eleven years old. She likes animals. She enjoys horse riding (on the beach).
Eric: Eric is 45 years old. He likes old cars. He enjoys driving.

c) **Zhen:** My name is Zhen. I am 40 years old. I like interesting old places. I enjoy English history.
Trevor: My name is Trevor. I am ten years old. I like the dirt and I have lots of fun. I enjoy mountain biking in the forest.

75 a) It is a picture of a **shoe** shop.
b) There is a **big** scorpion on the wall.
c) There are **two** shoes on the wall.
d) Scorpion is a **small** shop in London.
e) **There are two big signs on the wall of the shop.**
f) *(Musterlösung)*
Yes, I do. I like shopping in my town and I usually buy CDs. I like going shopping with my friends.
or:
No, I don't. I find shopping boring. I like playing tennis.

76 *individuelle Lösungen (Musterlösungen vgl. Beispiele)*

77 You: Where is the Seaview Fun Park?
Friend: It is in Newquay.
You: When is it open?
Friend: It is open from Monday to Saturday. It's closed on Sunday.
You: How much does it cost?

FRIEND: It is £ 5.50 for adults and £ 3.75 for children. / Adults pay £ 5.50 and children £ 3.75. / It costs adults £ 5.50 and children £ 3.75.
YOU: What are the opening times? / When is the fun park open?
FRIEND: It is open from 2 p.m. until 8 p.m.

Topic 45: The Eden Project

178 a) "What are you doing?"
"**I'm looking** at the Eden Project on the internet."

b) "**Are you here on holiday?**"
"Yes, I'm on holiday here. I come from Germany."

c) "Are you having a nice holiday in Cornwall?"
"**Yes, I am**. Thank **you**."

179 a) TOM: **Where is the Eden Project, Sally?**
SALLY: It's in Cornwall, England.

b) TOM: **What is the Eden Project?**
SALLY: It is a project about us, the climate and plants – a 'global garden'.
TOM: **What are the climates?**
SALLY: There are three – there is a Mediterranean dome and a rainforest dome, then outside there is the normal climate for Cornwall.
TOM: **What is in the domes?**
SALLY: Flowers, plants, bananas and lots of other things – the rainforest dome is very hot.

c) TOM: **How much is the Eden Project, Sally? / How much does the Eden Project cost, Sally?**
SALLY: £ 16 for adults and £ 5 for children.
TOM: **When is it open? /**
     When / What are the opening times?
SALLY: In summer, from 10 a.m. to 6 p.m.

80

YOU

Draw yourself (or: photo of you).

Write about yourself.
(Your name, age, where you come from, what you like doing, …)

My name is Mary Smith.
I am 12 years old.
I come from America.
I like reading and watching television.

Draw how you usually travel (or photo).

Draw your home (or photo).

What is a typical day for you? I wake up, eat my breakfast and then I go to school. I'm in / at school until 4 o'clock. Then I go home and do my homework. My evening meal is at 6.15 p.m. After that, I do some more homework, chat to my friends on the internet and listen to music. I go to bed at about 9.15 p.m.

What is your favourite food? spaghetti

What is your favourite drink? cola

What is your favourite thing? my dog

Bildnachweis

Umschlag: © Pashok/Dreamstime.com
S. 1: © Photowitch/Dreamstime.com
S. 2: © Martinmark/Dreamstime.com
S. 4: **Herrenhaus** © Paul Jenkinson, **Auto** © Mlan61/Dreamstime.com,
   Park © Michael Richert, RGBStock.com/www.sxc.hu
S. 9, 29, 105, 108 –114, 118, 130/131, 138, 150, 154, 252/253, 263: © Paul Jenkinson
S. 15/192: **Polaroid** © David Franklin/Dreamstime.com,
   Buchladen © Monkey Business Images/Dreamstime.com,
   Flugzeug © Emmanuel Wuyts/sxc.hu, **Flughafen** © fcl1971/sxc.hu, **Teddy** © mzacha/sxc.hu
S. 16: © Mikhail Basov/Dreamstime.com
S. 17: © Jeffrey Banke/Dreamstime.com
S. 21: © Ambrozjo/sxc.hu
S. 27: © Ljupco Smokovski/Dreamstime.com
S. 30/198: © Yuri Arcurs/Dreamstime.com
S. 33: **Mädchen** © Elena Elisseeva/Dreamstime.com,
   Junge © Denis Radovanovic/Dreamstime.com
S. 34/200: **Chloe** © Pavel Losevsky/Dreamstime.com,
   Laura, Jenny, Robert, Mike © Monkey Business Images/Dreamstime.com
S. 35/201: © Nikolai Sorokin/Dreamstime.com
S. 38: © Gemenacom/Dreamstime.com
S. 42: © Goran Stojanovic/Dreamstime.com
S. 43/207: © spekulator/sxc.hu
S. 47: © Fotograf: Mike Peel; http://commons.wikimedia.org/wiki/File:Snowshill_Manor _1.jpg;
   lizenziert unter der Creative Commons Attribution-Share Alike 2.5 Generic-Lizenz
S. 50: **A** © Feije Riemersma/Dreamstime.com, **B** © Eddy Van Ryckeghem/Dreamstime.com,
   C © Awie Badenhorst/Dreamstime.com, **D** © Carolyne Pehora/Dreamstime.com,
   E © Atm2003/Dreamstime.com, **F** © Marcus Miranda/Dreamstime.com
S. 53: **ältere Dame** © tbel/Fotolia.com, **Mädchen** © Justin Horrocks/www.istockphoto.com,
   Mann © Yuri Arcurs/Fotolia.com,
   A © iprole/sxc.hu, **B** © Patrycja Peslak/Dreamstime.com, **C** © Marjanneke/Dreamstime.com,
   D Coladose © Feng Yu/Dreamstime.com, **Geld** © Jiri Hera/Dreamstime.com,
   F © Frank Boston/Dreamstime.com, **G** © Ashestosky/Dreamstime.com,
   H © Davidwatmough/Dreamstime.com
S. 54: **Puzzleteil** © Pinzio/Dreamstime.com, **A** © Roman Milert/Dreamstime.com,
   B © Toxawww/Dreamstime.com, **C** © Rafael Angel Irusta Machin/Dreamstime.com,
   D © Czalewski/Dreamstime.com
S. 58/218: © Terence Mendoza/Dreamstime.com
S. 60: © Jack Hollingsworth/Dreamstime.com
S. 61: © Raja Rc/Dreamstime.com
S. 62: © Clare Matthews/sxc.hu
S. 64: © Ramona Smiers/Dreamstime.com
S. 65/227: **Katze** © Darrenw/Dreamstime.com, **Hotelschild** © Flynt/Dreamstime.com,
   Hotellobby © Kelvintt/Dreamstime.com
S. 67: © Amagraphic/Dreamstime.com
S. 69: **A** © Davide Guglielmo/www.sxc.hu, **B** Redaktion, **C** © Sergey Katykin/Dreamstime.com,
   D © Dreamstime.com, **E** © Bubbels/sxc.hu, **F** © Belu32/Dreamstime.com,
   G © Davide Guglielmo/www.sxc.hu, **H** © asifthebes/sxc.hu, **I** © drniels/sxc.hu
S. 71: © Loopall/Dreamstime.com
S. 78: **Karteikasten** © Linnell Esler/sxc.hu, **Karteikarte** © sleov/sxc.hu
S. 79: © sleov/sxc.hu
S. 81: **leeres Heft** © labarbosa/sxc.hu, **Karopapier** © nkzs/sxc.hu
S. 84: © Natalia Barsukova/Dreamstime.com
S. 86/240: **Rahmen** © Daniil Semenov/Dreamstime.com,
   Familie © Monkey Business Images/Dreamstime.com

Bildnachweis

S. 92: **A** © Rafael Angel Irusta Machin/Dreamstime.com, **B** © Oleksandr Kalyna/Dreamstime.com, **C** © Ferenc Ungor/Dreamstime.com, **D** © Photostouch/Dreamstime.com, **E** © Felinda/Dreamstime.com, **F** © Monsieurpix/Dreamstime.com
S. 98: **Katze** © Evgeny Dubinchuk/Dreamstime.com, **Welpe/Lamm/Fohlen** © Eric Isselée/Dreamstime.com
S. 101: © Rui Dias Aidos/Dreamstime.com
S. 103: **Handy** © Rasá Messina Francesca/Dreamstime.com, **Schmuck** © hksusp/sxc.hu, **Pommes** © jean scheijen/sxc.hu
S. 107: © Kbuconi/Dreamstime.com
S. 115: © Zoom-zoom/Dreamstime.com
S. 117: © Andres Rodriguez/Dreamstime.com
S. 119: © Jan van den Brink/Dreamstime.com
S. 120: **A** © Fotograf: Thomas Bredøl; http://commons.wikimedia.org/wiki/File:Trafalgar_Square _2004.jpg; lizenziert unter der Creative Commons Attribution 2.5 Denmark-Lizenz; **B–E** © Paul Jenkinson, **Polaroid** © David Franklin/Dreamstime.com
S. 121: © Temistocle Lucarelli/Dreamstime.com
S. 122: © frecuencia/sxc.hu
S. 123: © Rainer Claus/Fotolia.de
S. 124/259: © labarbosa/sxc.hu
S. 125: © Speedfighter17/Dreamstime.com
S. 126/262: © Evero333/Dreamstime.com
S. 129: © Jarenwicklund/Dreamstime.com
S. 146/268: © ilco/sxc.hu
S. 147: **Carmen** © Tina Baumgartner/Dreamstime.com, **Zhen** © Nam Fook Voon/Dreamstime.com, **Chloe/Eric** © Yuri Arcurs/Dreamstime.com, **Trevor** © Anton Albert/Dreamstime.com, **Dave** © Lucabertolli/Dreamstime.com
S. 148: **A–D, F** © Paul Jenkinson, **E** © Martinmark/Dreamstime.com
S. 151: **Mädchen** © Frenk and Danielle Kaufmann/Dreamstime.com, **Emoticons** © Vitaliy Rozhkov/Dreamstime.com, **Filmrolle** © Helder Monteiro/Dreamstime.com
S. 153: **Kettenkarussell** © mhunteer111/sxc.hu, **Luftballons** © Ashestosky/Dreamstime.com
S. 155: © Fotograf: Jürgen Matern, http://commons.wikimedia.org/wiki/File:Eden_Project_ geodesic_domes_panorama.jpg; lizenziert unter der Creative Commons Attribution-Share Alike 2.5-Lizenz
S. 156: **Pinnwand** © Paul Jenkinson, **Eden Project Innenansicht** © Fotograf: Stevekeiretsu, http://commons.wikimedia.org/wiki/File:Eden_ project_tropical_biome.jpg; lizenziert unter der Creative Commons Attribution 1.0 Generic-Lizenz
S. 183: © Michelle Robek/Dreamstime.com
S. 215: **ältere Dame** © tbel/Fotolia.com, **Mädchen** © Justin Horrocks/www.istockphoto.com, **Mann** © Yuri Arcurs/Fotolia.com
S. 233–235: **Karteikarte** © sleov/sxc.hu
S. 271: **Mädchen** © Elena Elisseeva/Dreamstime.com, **Schulbus** © Fotograf: AEMoreira042281, http://commons.wikimedia.org/wiki/File:First_ Student_USA_minibus_215516.jpg; lizenziert unter der GNU Free Documentation-Lizenz, Version 1.2,
Haus © Fotograf: EugeneZelenko, http://commons.wikimedia.org/wiki/File:USA-Saratoga-Van_Arsdale_House.jpg; lizenziert unter der GNU Free Documentation-Lizenz, Version 1.2,
Hintergrund © Fotograf: Stevekeiretsu, http://commons.wikimedia.org/wiki/File:Eden_ project_tropical_biome.jpg; lizenziert unter der Creative Commons Attribution 1.0 Generic-Lizenz
Digital: **Radio** © Jean Scheijen/sxc.hu, **Straße bei Nacht** © oriontrail. Shutterstock, **Junge mit Rucksack** © iodrakon. Shutterstock, **Fisch im Glas** © Danish Zaidi. Pearson India Education Services Pvt. Ltd,
Palette © Hayati Kayhan. Shutterstock;
alle übrigen Bilder und Zeichnungen: siehe obiger Bildnachweis

Liebe Kundin, lieber Kunde,

der STARK Verlag hat das Ziel, Sie effektiv beim Lernen zu unterstützen. In welchem Maße uns dies gelingt, wissen Sie am besten. Deshalb bitten wir Sie, uns Ihre Meinung zu den STARK-Produkten in dieser Umfrage mitzuteilen:

www.stark-verlag.de/feedback

Als Dankeschön verlosen wir einmal jährlich, zum 31. Juli, unter allen Teilnehmern ein aktuelles Samsung-Tablet. Für nähere Informationen und die Teilnahmebedingungen folgen Sie dem Internetlink.

Herzlichen Dank!

Haben Sie weitere Fragen an uns?
Sie erreichen uns telefonisch **0180 3 179000***
per E-Mail **info@stark-verlag.de**
oder im Internet unter **www.stark-verlag.de**

Lernen • Wissen • Zukunft

*9 Cent pro Min. aus dem deutschen Festnetz, Mobilfunk bis 42 Cent pro Min. Aus dem Mobilfunknetz wählen Sie die Festnetznummer: **08167 9573-0**

Erfolgreich durch alle Klassen mit den **STARK** Reihen

Training

Prüfungsrelevantes Wissen schülergerecht präsentiert. Übungsaufgaben mit Lösungen sichern den Lernerfolg.

Klassenarbeiten

Praxisnahe Übungen für eine gezielte Vorbereitung auf Klassenarbeiten.

STARK in Klassenarbeiten

Schülergerechtes Training wichtiger Themenbereiche für mehr Lernerfolg und bessere Noten.

Kompakt-Wissen

Kompakte Darstellung des prüfungsrelevanten Wissens zum schnellen Nachschlagen und Wiederholen.

VERA 8

Grundwissen mit Beispielen und Übungsaufgaben im Stil von VERA 8. Mit schülergerechten Lösungen.

Und vieles mehr auf www.stark-verlag.de

Pearson English Readers

Lektüren für verschiedene Niveaustufen zu spannenden Themen. Mit hilfreichen Worterklärungen.

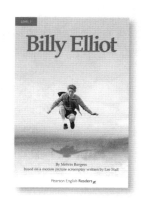

Alle Titel zu Pearson English Readers
www.stark-verlag.de/english-readers

Bestellungen bitte direkt an
STARK Verlagsgesellschaft mbH & Co. KG · Postfach 1852 · 85318 Freising
Tel. 0180 3 179000* · Fax 0180 3 179001* · www.stark-verlag.de · info@stark-verlag.de

Lernen ▪ Wissen ▪ Zukunft
STARK

*9 Cent pro Min. aus dem deutschen Festnetz, Mobilfunk bis 42 Cent pro Min. Aus dem Mobilfunknetz wählen Sie die Festnetznummer: **08167 9573-0**